IMPRINTS OF THE PAST:

THE JOURNEY TO SELF-AWARENESS AND RESILIENCE

BY CHANTER T. SIMMONS

Table of Contents

IMPRINTS OF THE PAST: THE JOURNEY TO SELF-AWARENESS AND RESILIENCE i
COPYRIGHT iii
DEDICATION iv
PREFACE v
INTRODUCTION vi
CHAPTER 1 viii
   The Hidden Footprints Of Yesterday 1
CHAPTER 2 7
   The Weight Of Silence 7
CHAPTER 3 9
   The Mirror Of Relationships 9
CHAPTER 4 20
   The Power of Self-Recognition 20
CHAPTER 5 28
   The Healing Power Of Self-Compassion: The Art Of Emotional Nurturing ... 28
CHAPTER 6 40
   Becoming the Architect of Your Healing 40
CHAPTER 7 51
   Integrating The New Self 51
CHAPTER 8 58
   The Becoming: Stepping Into Your Future Self 58
CHAPTER 9 66
   Walking In Your Becoming 66
CHAPTER 10 73
   Becoming The Author Of Your New Story 73
CHAPTER 11 79
   Closing: Stepping Into The Freedom You Have Created 79
EPILOGUE 80
ACKNOWLEDGMENTS 82
ABOUT THE AUTHOR 84

COPYRIGHT

Imprints of the Past: The Journey to Self-Awareness and Resilience

© 2025 by Chanter Simmons
All rights reserved.

No part of this publication may be reproduced, distributed, or transmitted in any form or by any means, including photocopying, recording, or other electronic or mechanical methods, without the prior written permission of the publisher, except in the case of brief quotations used in reviews or articles.

Published by Grace & Mercy Therapeutic Resolutions Publishing Printed in the United States of America

ISBN 979-8-9944247-0-4 First Edition – 2025

Cover design by Chanter T Simmons Interior layout by Chanter T. Simmons

Disclaimer: This book is intended for informational and inspirational purposes only. It is not a substitute for professional medical, mental health, or therapeutic advice. Readers should seek guidance from qualified professionals for any condition requiring diagnosis or treatment.

DEDICATION

To my first love for His Grace & Mercy that endures forever.

For my grandmother, whose love was my first lesson in belonging and whose voice still reminds me of how special I am. You taught me the power of legacy, who we are and what we build matters beyond our years. Your faith, strength, and wisdom continue to guide my steps, and this book is a reflection of that inheritance.

And for every person who has ever doubted their worth, may you discover in these pages that your story, too, carries purpose, strength, and grace.

PREFACE

We all carry stories that no one else can see. They live beneath our smiles, behind our decisions, and in the quiet moments when the world feels still. Some stories are beautiful reminders of love and growth. Others are wounds or scars left by betrayal, loss, or moments that changed who we believed we could be. These are the imprints of the past.

For years, I mistook survival for healing. I believed that as long as I kept moving forward, the pain would lose its power. But time does not heal what we refuse to acknowledge. The body remembers. The heart remembers. The mind protects, but protection without reflection becomes a prison. It took courage to stop running long enough to ask: *What am I carrying that no longer belongs to me?*

This book was born from that question.

Imprints of the Past: The Journey to Self-Awareness and Resilience is not about revisiting pain to relive it, it's about revisiting pain to release it. It is a journey inward, toward understanding how our histories have shaped our present and how awareness can set us free. Each chapter offers space for reflection, truth-telling, and rebuilding. The goal is not perfection, but presence—to become fully awake to who you are beneath what happened.

You may find pieces of yourself in these pages: the child who learned to be silent, the adult who learned to be strong, the soul that is learning to be whole. Healing is not about erasing the past; it's about learning to carry it differently. When we confront the weight of our memories with honesty and compassion, we begin to rise not in denial of what was, but in celebration of what still can be.

Your story matters. Your scars tell the truth about your strength. And every imprint, no matter how painful, can become the foundation of resilience. So, take a deep breath, open your heart, and step into your story. This is where the rising begins.

INTRODUCTION

Introduction – Imprints of the Past: The Journey to Self-Awareness and Resilience

Everyone carries something they rarely speak of, a shadow, a memory, a moment that quietly shaped who they became. For some, it's a voice that once said, *"You'll never be enough."* For others, it's an experience so heavy that silence felt safer than acknowledgment. But the truth is this: what we don't confront eventually begins to confront us. Our past has a way of echoing through our choices, our relationships, and our sense of self until we finally stop and listen.

How do we move toward success when the voices of our past still whisper words of doubt, casting long shadows over our confidence and identity? That question haunted me for years. Was what I'd been told about myself true? Should I even try to become the person I envisioned? Was I truly enough? I didn't realize that I had become more loyal to my fears than to my purpose. My doubts had become comfortable companions always there to remind me of my limits, rarely allowing me to imagine my potential. Eventually, I reached a breaking point where surviving was no longer enough. I wanted to live, to thrive, to step into the version of myself that I could finally be proud of. And that meant confronting the imprints of my past.

The Stories We Carry

We all have stories that shaped us, others told to us, others talked about us, and a few we silently told ourselves. These stories become internal maps, guiding how we see the world and our place within it. When those stories are rooted in pain, disappointment, or rejection, they can distort our self-image. We begin to measure our worth through the lens of what hurt us, instead of who we truly are.

Many of us were never taught that healing begins with awareness. We move through life trying to outrun what we've endured, believing that if we work hard enough, smile often enough, or appear successful enough, the past will lose its grip. But avoidance is not healing—it's delay. Every unaddressed wound waits for acknowledgment. It whispers through insecurity, fear of intimacy, perfectionism, and the inability to rest. Healing doesn't ask us to forget; it asks us to finally see.

The Invisible Imprints

Unresolved trauma is not always dramatic or obvious. Sometimes it hides in our daily patterns the way we over-apologize, overwork, or avoid vulnerability. These are the invisible imprints of the past: subtle emotional fingerprints that shape our identity, behavior, and relationships.

Maybe you grew up believing that love had to be earned, or that vulnerability invited rejection. Maybe you learned to silence your emotions because no one seemed to hear them. These experiences don't vanish when we become adults, they evolve. They follow us into careers, marriages, parenting, and self-perception. They influence how much success we believe we deserve and how much joy we allow ourselves to experience.

This book does not exist to blame the past but to understand it. When we identify the patterns born from pain, we gain the power to rewrite them. Healing is not about reliving your story—it's about reclaiming authorship of it.

The Journey Toward Self-Awareness

Self-awareness is the bridge between pain and purpose. It asks us to pause and look within, even when what we see feels uncomfortable. It challenges us to ask: *Where did this belief about myself come from? Who taught me to think this way? What might change if I released it?*

For me, awareness began the moment I realized that fear had become my compass. Every decision I made was filtered through the possibility of failure or rejection. I was living reactively, not intentionally. The first step toward change was honestly admitting that my past was influencing my present more than I wanted to believe. That acknowledgment opened the door to something greater: freedom.

Awareness alone doesn't heal, but it awakens the desire to heal. It reminds us that we have choices, even if the past didn't give us many. It invites us to stop surviving and start creating, to trade old narratives for new truths.

From Surviving to Rising

Resilience isn't born in comfort; it's forged in challenge. But true resilience isn't just about enduring hardship, it's about transforming it. Many of us were taught to "be strong," but strength without self-understanding can turn into numbness. The goal is not to harden against pain, but to soften into wisdom.

Rising beyond the past doesn't mean pretending it never happened. It means recognizing that what once broke you can now build you. Every scar tells a story of survival, but healing allows that story to evolve into one of purpose. Your greatest pain can become your greatest teacher if you are willing to listen.

What You'll Discover in These Pages

Imprints of the Past: The Journey to Self-Awareness and Resilience is both a reflection and a roadmap. Each chapter explores a stage of awakening from recognizing emotional imprints, to releasing self-defeating patterns, to rebuilding identity and resilience.

You'll be invited to look inward through guided questions, stories, and exercises designed to help you:

- Identify how past experiences shape your present choices.
- Recognize emotional patterns that no longer serve you.
- Cultivate awareness, self-compassion, and purpose.
- Transform pain into growth and resilience.

This is not a quick-fix guide or a collection of motivational quotes it's an invitation to do the deeper work. Healing is not linear, and it's not perfect. Some days you'll feel progress; other days you'll revisit familiar pain. But each step, no matter how small, is movement toward freedom.

The Invitation to Heal

You cannot heal what you refuse to face but facing it transforms everything. The moment you begin to confront your truth, your healing begins. The past may have written the first chapters of your story, but you hold the pen now.

As you move through these pages, give yourself permission to feel, to reflect, and to release. Be patient with your process. Healing is not about erasing what was it's about learning to carry it differently.

Step out of the shadows of the past and into the light of who you truly are. The road ahead may be uncertain, but it leads to resilience, wholeness, and freedom. This is your moment to rise beyond the imprints of the past and reclaim the power of your own becoming.

CHAPTER 1
The Hidden Footprints of Yesterday

The past is never truly gone; it lingers alive in our habits, fears, and the emotions that surface when we least expect them. It speaks in subtle ways: in the tension we feel when someone raises their voice, in the hesitation before we trust, and in the quiet ache that follows certain memories. These fragments of experience shape how we move through the world. They form the framework through which we perceive reality.

We often believe that once a moment has passed, it no longer holds power over us. Yet the truth is more complex. The mind records, the body remembers, and the heart holds what words cannot express. Every choice, every reaction, every emotional reflex carries traces of what came before. The past does not disappear it transforms into patterns that quietly guide the present.

Our habits, fears, and emotional responses become the lens through which we view life. They influence how we interpret love, failure, and possibility. When we face new challenges, we do not approach them as blank slates; we approach them as the sum of every experience that came before. Some of those experiences empower us, reminding us of our strength. Others distort our reflection, whispering that we are not enough.

The process of healing and self-discovery begins with recognizing that these inner voices are echoes, not prophecies. The moment we understand that our reactions are not random but rooted in memory, we reclaim the ability to choose differently. Awareness transforms reaction into response.

The Power of Self-Awareness

Self-awareness is more than a concept; it is a courageous act. It is the ability to look inward without judgment and to see ourselves with clarity and compassion. It requires honesty about how we feel, how we behave, and why we do the things we do.

Most of us spend years operating on emotional autopilot. We say yes when we mean no. We withdraw instead of communicating. We chase validation while fearing rejection. We repeat cycles that frustrate us, wondering why change feels impossible. Without awareness, however, we fail to recognize that our behavior is the visible expression of invisible imprints.

True self-awareness begins with curiosity. It is not about perfection or guilt; it is about inquiry. It invites us to ask: Where did this pattern come from? Why do I react this way? What emotion am I protecting myself from? Each "why" becomes a doorway to deeper understanding.

The practice of self-awareness allows us to own both our progress and our pain. It reminds us that we are not defined by what happened to us but shaped by how we respond to it. In awareness, there is power, because awareness creates choice. When we understand ourselves, we can interrupt the cycles that keep us stuck and consciously rewrite the narrative of who we are becoming.

The Healing in Asking "Why"

Every journey toward healing begins with a question. The simple act of asking "why" turns pain into purpose. Why do I feel anxious in stillness? Why do I need to prove my worth? Why do I struggle to trust? These questions are not accusations; they are invitations. Each one draws truth from the shadows and brings it into the light.

The question "why" is the language of transformation. It moves us from blame to understanding. It shifts us from being victims of circumstances to participants in our own evolution. When we ask why, we begin to see that our triggers are teachers, our discomforts are clues, and our emotions are messengers guiding us toward what needs attention.

Healing is not about erasing the past, but about learning from it. It is the process of revisiting the parts of ourselves we have avoided and choosing to see them differently. When we approach our pain with compassion rather than shame, we allow ourselves to grow through it. The "why" guides this process it turns confusion into clarity and chaos into meaning.

To heal is to become fluent in your own emotional language. It is to recognize that your body, your reactions, and your instincts are all speaking truths shaped by experiences you may have forgotten but never fully released. Asking "why" is how we begin to translate those truths.

The Awakening

As we learn to ask "why," we awaken to the realization that our past no longer has to define us. What once controlled us becomes something we can understand, honor, and release. Awareness becomes the key that unlocks freedom, and healing becomes the path that leads us home to ourselves.

The footprints of yesterday will always exist, but they no longer have to dictate where you walk tomorrow. The past can inform without imprisoning, teach without limiting, and remind without restraining.

Each time you pause to ask "why," you reclaim a piece of your power. Every moment of awareness is an act of healing, and every choice to face yourself with honesty becomes a quiet revolution, a decision to rise beyond what was and step fully into what can be.

The Stories We Never Told

Some of the most defining moments of our lives are the ones we never speak about, not because they lacked significance, but because their weight felt too heavy for words. These are the stories we tuck away in the corners of our hearts, the memories we whisper to no one, not even ourselves.

We often choose silence because it feels safer than truth. We convince ourselves that if we bury a memory deeply enough, the feelings attached to it will eventually fade. But silence does not dissolve our experiences; it preserves them. The pain we try to hide becomes the pain that lives quietly within us.

Many of us learned early that vulnerability was dangerous. Perhaps we were met with disbelief when we tried to speak. Perhaps our feelings were minimized, dismissed, or punished. Or perhaps no one ever created a space where our truth felt welcome. And so, we learned to hold our breath, swallow our emotions, and move forward as if nothing had happened.

But the body remembers what the mind tries to forget.

The stories we suppress linger in our reactions, insecurities, hesitations, and fears. They shape the way we love, influence the boundaries we set, and affect the trust we struggle to give.

Unspoken stories become emotional ghosts, not visible, yet always present.

They haunt our choices, shape our expectations, and whisper reminders of what once hurt us. When these stories remain hidden, they form barriers between who we are and who we are trying to become.

And perhaps the saddest truth is this: every untold story carries a piece of us with it.

When we silence our experiences, we silence parts of our identity. We silence the child who needed comfort, the teenager who needed understanding, and the adult who needed permission to feel. We silence the version of ourselves that needed compassion, honesty, and release.

But healing cannot grow in the dark.

It begins with acknowledgment, not public confession, not reliving every wound, but simply saying to yourself:

"This happened. And it mattered."

Naming the story is the first step toward reclaiming the power it took from you.

Finding the Courage to Break the Silence

Breaking silence is not easy. It requires a kind of courage that isn't loud or dramatic, but quiet, steady, and deeply personal. It is the courage to face yourself honestly, to acknowledge what hurt you, and to give your own emotions the respect they deserve all along.

For many of us, speaking our truth feels dangerous because, at some point in our lives, it was. We learned that expressing pain could invite rejection, ridicule, or punishment. We learned to hold back tears because someone told us emotions made us weak. We learned to pretend, to perform, to push through, all while our hearts quietly begged for permission to feel.

Finding your voice is not about forcing yourself to relive the past; it is about allowing your truth to exist.

Breaking silence doesn't always require an audience.

It doesn't require confrontation.

It doesn't require a perfect moment or the right words.

It simply requires you.

It begins with speaking gently to yourself, acknowledging the memories you've tucked away and giving them space to breathe. It begins with saying things like, "That hurt me," "I deserved better," "I am allowed to feel this," or "This experience shaped me, but it does not define me." Each of these statements is a doorway to healing. Each one chips away at the walls silence built around your heart.

Finding the courage to break the silence also means taking small, manageable steps that gently move you toward truth. It may begin with writing your feelings in a journal, even if it's only one sentence at a time, simply to give your emotions a place to land. It can look like confiding in a trusted friend or speaking with a therapist who can hold space for what you've carried alone. Sometimes it means sitting in prayer or meditation and allowing emotions to rise without shutting them down. Other times, it's the quiet admission to yourself that you are tired of carrying what was never meant to be carried in silence.

Courage grows in moments, not leaps.

It grows each time honesty replaces avoidance, each time you choose to feel instead of suppressing, and each time you allow yourself to be fully human.

The moment you begin to give voice to your pain you reclaim power from your past. You loosen the grip of shame, silence, and fear. You step into a version of yourself that honors truth over performance and healing over hiding.

Breaking the silence isn't about revisiting old wounds.

It's about choosing not to live from them anymore.

The Freedom in Expression

Expression is the bridge between silence and healing. When we allow ourselves to speak, whether through words, writing, prayer, or honest self-reflection, we create space for release. Expression is not about reliving pain; it is about letting it go. It is the gentle untangling of emotions that have been knotted deep within us for years.

Many of us were taught that expressing our emotions makes us dramatic, difficult, or weak. We learned to keep our voices low, our needs small, and our feelings tucked away. But expression is not a flaw; it is a fundamental part of being human. Our voices were given to us for connection, clarity, and truth.

The moment we begin to express what we feel, even if it sounds messy, imperfect, or unfinished, something begins to shift within us. We reclaim parts of ourselves we abandoned to keep the peace. We reconnect with emotions we once numbed. We rediscover the permission to be honest about where we hurt and what we desire.

Expression brings freedom because it allows us to release what no longer belongs inside.

Emotional expression can take many forms. Sometimes freedom sounds like a whispered confession: "I'm tired." Other times, it looks like tears we've held back for years. It might be writing in a journal until the pages feel lighter or speaking truths aloud during prayer. It could be sharing your story with someone you trust or simply acknowledging your feelings to yourself without shame.

What matters is not how you express yourself, but that you allow expression to happen.

Silence keeps pain trapped; expression gives it somewhere to go.

When you begin to express what you've buried, something powerful happens. The weight on your chest slowly begins to lift, and the mind that once felt overwhelmed starts to quiet. Your emotions become clearer, easier to understand, and less intimidating. Even your body begins to relax, releasing tension it has held for far too long. Most importantly, you begin to feel a deep sense of alignment between who you are on the inside and the life you are trying to live on the outside.

Expression reconnects you with your truth.

It is the doorway back to yourself.

With every word, tear, line of writing, or moment of honesty, you reclaim a piece of your identity the piece that silence tried to take. You step deeper into emotional freedom and closer to the resilience you are building, chapter by chapter, truth by truth.

Stepping Into Your Emotional Truth

Stepping into your emotional truth often requires peeling back layers of identity we build for protection. For years, I prided myself on being someone who kept things "real." I carried a reputation for being direct, honest, and grounded in realistic perspectives. I believed that this toughness, this version of authenticity, was enough to count as emotional awareness. In my mind, being straightforward meant I was in tune with myself.

But realism and emotional truth are not the same.

My outer presentation was confident, carefree, and to the point, but internally, I was struggling. Beneath my straightforward demeanor lived a quiet battle I rarely acknowledged. I believed I wasn't good enough, not smart enough, not pretty enough, not special enough. And because I refused to speak these truths aloud, they began to define me. My silence became fertile ground for depression, self-doubt, and poor self-efficacy. I looked strong on the outside while privately wrestling with narratives that chipped away at my sense of identity.

It took time, and honesty, to realize that "keeping it real" meant nothing if I wasn't willing to be real with myself. Pretending to be unaffected only deepened the disconnect between who I was and who I wanted to become.

True emotional truth requires more than toughness; it requires tenderness.

CHAPTER 2
The Weight of Silence

Silence Has a Sound. It hums beneath conversations, hides behind smiles, and echoes in the pauses we're afraid to fill. For many of us, silence becomes a survival tool a way to protect ourselves from judgment, rejection, or pain. Yet what once shielded us can just as easily imprison us.

We go through life muting the traumas we experience, hoping that someone will one day look close enough to notice the hurt we've hidden. We hope they will recognize our disappointments, understand our unspoken fears, and care enough to reassure us that the pain buried beneath those muted traumas will eventually soften and fade. In that longing, we silence ourselves further waiting for healing to come from the outside, when it must begin within.

We often tell ourselves that if we don't speak it, we won't feel it. But silence doesn't erase what hurts; it only buries it alive. The emotions we suppress don't disappear, they wait. They wait in the tension in our shoulders, the heaviness in our chest, the irritability we can't explain, and the exhaustion that lingers even after rest. The unspoken becomes the unseen weight we carry into every room we enter.

In my own life, I once believed that silence was strength. I thought that if I could hold everything in the sadness, the disappointment, the confusion I could control it. But in believing that silence was strength, I unknowingly delayed my healing and stunted my emotional growth. What I didn't realize was that silence doesn't protect peace; it prevents healing. It keeps us surviving instead of living. It took years for me to understand that giving voice to pain doesn't make you weak, it makes you whole.

The Cost of Silence

Silence always comes at a cost. It may feel protective in the moment, but over time, it carves hollow spaces within us. When we silence our pain, we also silence our needs, our dreams, and our ability to be fully seen. We shrink ourselves to fit within the confines of what we believe others can handle. We learn to live small, even when our spirit was designed to live large.

Unspoken emotions don't vanish they grow heavier. The longer we carry them, the more they shape us. We become experts at appearing "okay" while quietly struggling beneath the weight of unresolved wounds. We smile to avoid questions, stay busy to avoid thinking, and care for others to avoid facing what we need for ourselves.

Silence becomes a language of its own a language of avoidance, fear, and exhaustion. Left unaddressed, it reshapes us from the inside out. It can turn into emotional numbness, making it difficult to feel joy or genuine connection. Silence creates inner conflict, where the truth of who we are battles against the version of ourselves we present to the world. It often fuels overthinking and anxiety, as the emotions we refuse to express find other ways to demand attention. Silence can lead to people-pleasing, causing us to sacrifice authenticity in exchange for approval. In many cases, it becomes self-sabotage a desperate attempt to outrun the very wounds we are afraid to face.

Whatever emotional traumas we refuse to release have no choice but to manifest in other areas of our lives. They show up in our relationships, in our reactions, in our fears, and even in our bodies. Suppressed pain leaks into the cracks of everyday life, in the way we love, in the way we trust, and in the way we see ourselves.

The irony is that silence begins as a shield but slowly becomes a cage. The longer we live inside that cage, the more we convince ourselves that we belong there.

The cost is also physical. The body listens, even when the mind refuses to speak. Stress accumulates in our muscles. Grief lingers in our breathing. Fear echoes in our heartbeat. The body keeps what we bury. It remembers what silence tries to forget.

When we do not release what pains us, our bodies are forced to carry the burden. But we were never meant to carry it alone. Nor were we meant to carry it forever.

CHAPTER 3
The Mirror of Relationships

Relationships reveal parts of ourselves we don't always notice. They reflect our fears, insecurities, hopes, and hidden wounds. Every connection, whether romantic, familial, or friendly, holds up a mirror, showing us who we believe we are and what we subconsciously feel we deserve.

We often assume that relationships begin with the other person, but in truth, they begin with us. We carry our histories into every interaction, the lessons we learned, the habits we formed, and the beliefs we never questioned. The past travels with us, shaping how we love, how we trust, and how we respond when we feel threatened or unseen.

Without realizing it, we recreate familiar emotional environments, even when they hurt us. If we grew up feeling unseen, we may find ourselves drawn to people who overlook us. If we learned to earn love, we may gravitate toward relationships where we must constantly prove our worth. If we experienced inconsistency or instability, we may normalize chaos and call it passion.

Relationships show us what still needs healing.

The people we attract and the dynamics we repeat are rarely accidents; they are emotional patterns playing out in real time. Our triggers become teachers, our conflicts become opportunities, and our connections become reflections of our inner world.

The uncomfortable truth is this:

Sometimes it's not the relationship that wounds us, it's the wound that chooses the relationship.

Many of us enter relationships carrying unspoken expectations. We hope others will fill the voids we never addressed, validate the worth we never claimed, or heal the pain we never confronted. But healing does not come from another person's presence; it comes from our own awareness.

In this chapter, we will explore how our past influences whom we choose, what we accept, how we love, and what we fear, along with the hidden parts of ourselves that only surface in connection with others. Understanding these patterns is not about placing blame but about gaining awareness, because once we see our relational patterns clearly, we finally have the power to break them. This awareness marks the beginning of relational healing: the moment we stop expecting relationships to save us and instead allow them to reveal, refine, and strengthen us.

Attachment Patterns: How Our Past Shapes How We Love

The way we love is never accidental. Long before we entered adult relationships, we learned how to connect, and how to protect ourselves from the people who raised us, cared for us, or failed to do so. Our earliest relationships created emotional blueprints, teaching us what love felt like, what safety looked like, and whether our needs were worth meeting. These patterns don't vanish with age; they follow us into every relationship we form.

The Secure Blueprint

When we grow up feeling supported, valued, and emotionally safe, we learn that connection is reliable. People with secure attachment tend to trust easily, communicate openly, and believe in mutual give-and-take. They understand that conflicts can be resolved and that love can be both stable and nurturing.

The Anxious Blueprint

If love in childhood felt inconsistent or unpredictable, we may develop an anxious attachment style. We become hyperaware of subtle changes, constantly fearing abandonment before it even occurs. We worry about being "too much," "not enough," or suddenly replaceable. Love becomes something we chase, fear losing, and cling to even when it causes us pain.

The Avoidant Blueprint

If closeness ever feels overwhelming, unsafe, or suffocating, we may learn to keep an emotional distance. We protect ourselves by remaining independent, self-reliant, and guarded. The avoidant pattern convinces us that needing someone is a weakness, prompting us to detach before anyone can get too close or risk disappointing us.

The Disorganized Blueprint

For those who have experienced trauma or unpredictable caregiving, attachment can feel confusing or conflicted. Love becomes both desired and feared. People with disorganized attachment often swing between wanting closeness and avoiding it, longing for connection but struggling to trust it.

These patterns are not character flaws; they are emotional survival strategies; tools developed in environments where we did the best we could with what we had. While these patterns once protected us, they may now prevent us from forming healthy, supportive connections.

Blueprints are often seen as rigid structures, fixed plans with little room for change. But unlike architectural blueprints, emotional ones are not permanent. When we examine our attachment styles, we discover that we have the power to redraw the lines, reinterpret the design, and recreate what connection looks like for us now. Healing invites us to revise what once felt unchangeable.

I've often been regarded as someone who gravitates toward isolation and solitude. On the surface, that can be misinterpreted as a negative trait. But contrary to that assumption, solitude has been a profound source of strength for me. It has given me the space to reflect, regroup, and reconnect with my own identity without the noise of external expectations. In solitude, I've found clarity and direction, the kind that gets lost when life becomes crowded with distractions and emotional clutter. What others may see as withdrawal has sometimes been my pathway to grounding, creativity, and inner peace.

Recognizing this helped me realize that not every relational pattern is a wound. Some patterns are strengths. Some are intentional choices. Some are coping strategies that helped us survive but now deserve to evolve. Knowing the difference allows us to rewrite our emotional blueprints with intention, compassion, and wisdom.

When you begin to understand your attachment blueprint, you gain the ability to change how you show up in relationships. Instead of reacting from old wounds, you learn to respond with clarity and intention. Communication becomes more open and honest rather than withdrawing or shutting down. You start to set boundaries from a place of self-respect instead of shrinking to keep the peace. You seek connections that nourish you rather than repeating familiar dysfunction. Ultimately, you choose love from a place of awareness and strength rather than fear or insecurity.

Awareness turns patterns into choices, and choices allow healing.

Triggers and Emotional Reflexes in Relationships

Every relationship carries moments that stir something deep inside us, moments that feel bigger than the situation itself. These emotional reactions are known as triggers, and they are among the clearest signs of where our healing still resides.

A trigger is not about what is happening now; it is a reaction shaped by what has happened before. It is the past tapping us on the shoulder, asking to be acknowledged.

Triggers reveal far more than the moment that activates them. They uncover what we fear losing, what we long for, what we never received, and what still feels unhealed. The intensity of our reaction is rarely about the relationship itself; it is a message from the wound beneath the surface.

Triggers feel powerful because they bypass logic. They activate the emotional memory system, the part of us that remembers the feeling of the wound even when the conscious mind cannot recall its origin. When someone behaves in a way that echoes an old emotional experience, the body reacts long before the mind catches up. A delayed text can stir abandonment fears. A simple question can trigger defensiveness. Silence can provoke panic. Honesty can awaken shame. Closeness can spark fear. These reactions are not who we are, they are echoes of what we learned to feel in order to survive.

Alongside these triggers are our emotional reflexes, automatic responses shaped by old patterns. These reflexes function like emotional muscle memory, happening quickly and without conscious awareness. For some, they look like shutting down to avoid vulnerability. For others, defensiveness hides feelings of inadequacy. Overexplaining becomes a shield against perceived rejection. Withdrawal protects us from conflict or overwhelms. Over-accommodating attempts to preserve connection at the cost of self. These responses are not intentional; they are conditioned protections. But what once kept us safe may now keep us stuck.

Reflecting on my own experiences with triggers, I recall moments when self-doubt surfaced instantly, especially when criticism felt personal or harsh, often from my parents. Their words reinforced a distorted view I already held of myself. In those moments, I didn't feel safe, supported, or wanted. The emotional weight intensified my depression and deepened my sense of hopelessness. As these patterns repeated, I recognized how much they were shaping my internal world. I realized I needed to confront these triggers rather than allow them to pull me back into familiar, low places. Challenging those old narratives became one of the first steps toward reclaiming my confidence and healing my self-worth.

Every trigger carries an opportunity for growth. It highlights the areas of our emotional blueprint ready for healing. Each trigger is an invitation to pause and ask:

Why did this moment feel so big?

What belief or memory is this awakening?

Is my reaction about now — or then?

What do I need to feel safe and grounded?

When we meet triggers with self-awareness, they cease to be explosive reactions and instead become valuable information. They guide us toward understanding our inner world, our relational patterns, and the healing we are still deserving of.

Recognizing When Familiar Isn't Healthy

One of the most challenging parts of healing is learning to recognize when something feels familiar, not because it is good for us, but because it mirrors an old wound. The human mind is drawn to what it knows, even when what it knows is painful. Familiarity can feel comforting, predictable, and easier to accept than the uncertainty of something new. But familiar does not always mean safe, and comfortable does not always mean healthy.

We often repeat emotional patterns not because they serve us, but because they resemble the environments in which we learned to survive. If chaos was normal, stability may feel threatening. If neglect was familiar, attention may feel overwhelming. If criticism was constant, love may feel undeserved. Unhealed experiences quietly shape our choices, pulling us back into dynamics that reflect our emotional history rather than our emotional needs.

The danger lies in mistaking recognition for connection. When someone reminds us of a parent, a past relationship, or an environment we once knew, it can create a false sense of closeness. The familiar energy feels like "home," even when "home" was the place where we learned to doubt ourselves, silence our needs, or tolerate emotional discomfort. We tell ourselves, "This feels right," or "This feels normal," or "This feels like love," without realizing that what feels right is often just what we know not what we deserve.

Unhealthy familiarity can show up in countless subtle ways: being drawn to partners who emotionally resemble a parent who hurt you, mistaking intensity for intimacy, feeling responsible for other people's emotions, accepting behaviors that make you shrink or question your worth, confusing inconsistency with passion, repeating cycles of abandonment or criticism, or feeling uneasy when relationships are peaceful because chaos feels more natural. When these patterns repeat, it is not a sign of failure, it is a sign of unhealed pain calling for attention.

We gravitate toward the familiar because the brain is wired for predictability. It prefers painful certainty over unknown possibility. The nervous system becomes accustomed to certain emotional rhythms, whether nurturing or not. So, when we encounter people or situations that mirror our past, the body responds with recognition, a deceptive sense of safety. Familiarity can feel like belonging, even when it keeps us bound to cycles that fracture our self-worth.

For me, recognizing the difference between familiar and healthy required brutal honesty. There were times in my life when I mistook emotional turbulence for passion because that was the model I had witnessed growing up. I believed love came with tension, inconsistency, or the need to earn my place. When relationships mirrored those patterns, they didn't alarm me, they felt normal. It took intentional self-awareness to understand that normal is not the same as nurturing.

Breaking the familiar pattern begins with questioning your instinctive yes. It requires asking yourself why you are drawn to certain people and whether the dynamic feels familiar or healthy. It involves exploring whether you are choosing relationships that align with your growth or ones that fit your wounds and determining whether the part of you that feels seen is your healed self or your hurt self. These questions do more than interrupt old habits, they reveal the truth beneath them.

Recognizing when familiar isn't healthy is a powerful act of self-protection. It is the moment you stop accepting emotional environments that wound you simply because you've been in them before. It is the moment you begin choosing relationships that reinforce your worth, not your wounds. Healing requires courage, the courage to break the cycle, the courage to choose differently, and the courage to walk away from what feels familiar but fractures your spirit.

The moment you choose yourself over familiar pain, you begin building a new emotional home, one rooted in peace, clarity, and self-respect.

Recognizing when the familiar isn't healthy is a powerful act of self-protection. It is the moment you stop accepting emotional environments that wound you simply because you've known them the longest. It is the moment you begin choosing relationships that reinforce your worth, not your wounds. Healing requires courage, the courage to break the cycle, the courage to choose differently, and the courage to walk away from what feels familiar but fractures your spirit.

As you build this new emotional home, it may not feel familiar at first. Stepping into healthier patterns often brings waves of anxiety, moments of isolation, and feelings of loneliness. These emotions are not signs that you are on the wrong path; they are simply the byproducts of renovation. Your mind and body are adjusting to a reality they have never known but deeply deserve.

Change often feels uncomfortable before it feels empowering.

But the reward emotional freedom, inner peace, and healthier connections is worth every moment of discomfort. Every step toward this new foundation is a declaration that you are choosing yourself, your healing, and your future over the weight of your past.

Building Emotional Safety — Creating Relationships That Support Your Healing

Once we recognize the patterns that no longer serve us, the question becomes: What does a healthy relationship actually look and feel like? For many of us, emotional safety wasn't modeled in childhood or early relationships. As a result, we may crave connection while simultaneously fearing it. We may desire healthy love but feel unprepared to receive it.

Emotional safety is not just a concept it is the foundation upon which every healthy connection is built. It is the experience of being with someone who allows you to be your full self without fear of punishment, abandonment, or ridicule. In an emotionally safe relationship, you can express your thoughts, needs, and boundaries without having to shrink, perform, or apologize for existing.

Emotional safety begins with three key elements: trust, consistency, and respect.

Trust allows vulnerability.

Consistency builds stability.

Respect protects dignity.

Together, these elements form the emotional ground where healing can take root.

Healthy relationships offer a different kind of familiarity, one built on peace rather than chaos, clarity rather than confusion, and acceptance rather than fear. They allow room for honest conversation, mistakes, growth, and emotional truth. They do not require you to sacrifice your needs to maintain connection.

But emotional safety is not created by the relationship alone, it is also shaped by the safety we cultivate within ourselves. You cannot experience safety externally if your internal world is ruled by fear, shame, or emotional doubt. Healing invites us to build a relationship with ourselves that reflects the care and compassion we seek from others.

Emotional safety also requires courage, the courage to stand up for yourself, honor your voice, and protect your peace, even when it feels unfamiliar. As your internal stability grows, emotion-driven reactions begin to soften, gradually replaced by reasoning, clarity, and spiritual alignment. The frantic need to defend or prove yourself gives way to a quieter, calmer, and more grounded version of you. Peace begins to take the place of confusion, and acceptance becomes a welcomed visitor rather than a distant hope.

We learn to ask for what we need instead of hoping someone will guess.

We learn to communicate our feelings instead of burying them.

We learn to honor our boundaries instead of abandoning them for approval.

We learn to choose people who respect us rather than those who mirror our wounds.

This shift doesn't happen overnight. It unfolds slowly and intentionally through small moments of honesty, self-reflection, and courage.

Emotional safety also involves unlearning the belief that love must be earned. Many of us carry this belief from childhood into our adult relationships, convincing ourselves that affection, attention, or stability must be earned. But healing teaches us that real love is not conditional, it is reciprocal. It expands, it supports, and it invites growth without demanding self-sacrifice.

When emotional safety becomes a priority, you begin to notice the difference between relationships that drain you and those that nourish you. You become more attuned to the energy you accept and the environments you allow yourself to inhabit. You stop chasing people who make you feel unseen and start gravitating toward those who honor your presence.

The more emotionally safe you become within yourself, the less likely you are to tolerate relationships that threaten your peace. As you strengthen your emotional foundation, you naturally attract connections that align with your healing rather than your history.

Boundaries — Loving Yourself Enough to Say No

Boundaries are one of the greatest acts of self-love, yet they are often the most challenging to practice. Many of us grew up believing that saying "no" was disrespectful, selfish, or unkind. We learned to prioritize the needs of others while silencing our own. Over time, this pattern conditions us to accept discomfort as normal and to confuse self-sacrifice with love.

But boundaries are not walls, they are doorways. They determine what enters your life and what no longer has permission to stay. A healthy boundary is not meant to punish others; it is meant to protect your peace. It communicates what you need in order to feel emotionally safe, respected, and valued. Boundaries create a structure in relationships that prevents resentment, burnout, and emotional overextension.

Loving yourself enough to say no means recognizing that your emotional well-being is non-negotiable. It means understanding that you cannot pour from an empty cup, nor can you build healthy connections when you constantly override your limits. Boundaries may initially feel uncomfortable, especially if you are used to pleasing others or avoiding conflict. The guilt that surfaces is not a sign that you are doing something wrong, it is simply the discomfort of breaking an old pattern. With practice, boundaries become easier, more natural, and deeply empowering.

Saying no might mean declining a request that drains you, stepping back from situations that feel misaligned, asking for clarity before responding, or calling out behavior that crosses your limits. Sometimes, it is as simple as affirming that you do not owe an explanation for choosing yourself. Setting boundaries is not about forcing others to change; it is about establishing a standard for how you allow yourself to be treated. The right people will respect your boundaries, while the wrong people will reveal themselves when you set them. In that revelation, you gain emotional freedom.

Emotional Accountability Taking Ownership of Your Inner World

Healthy relationships require accountability, not blame, not perfection, but the willingness to own your part in how you show up emotionally. This accountability is not rooted in shame; it is grounded in awareness. It means recognizing the difference between reacting from old wounds and responding from a place of healed clarity. Emotional accountability calls you to notice when a trigger is speaking instead of the present moment, when fear shapes your reactions, when past hurt influences your behavior, and when your communication is affected by unhealed pain.

It also means being willing to acknowledge when you have caused harm, whether intentionally or unintentionally, and addressing it with honesty and humility. Accountability strengthens relationships because it fosters emotional transparency. It removes guesswork and creates space for genuine understanding. When both individuals take responsibility for their emotions and actions, communication becomes clearer, trust deepens, and healing becomes a shared experience rather than a silent struggle.

Being accountable does not mean blaming yourself for everything or accepting mistreatment. It does not mean ignoring your needs or silencing your truth. Instead, it is a balanced practice of self-awareness and honesty. It recognizes that healing requires active participation, that emotional maturity grows through reflection, not avoidance. When you hold yourself accountable, you shift from living in reaction to living with intention. You stop repeating unconscious patterns and begin breaking them with purpose. In that shift, you take ownership of your emotional life, one of the greatest forms of empowerment.

G. Closing the Chapter Your Reflection in the Mirror

Relationships are mirrors, sometimes gentle, sometimes harsh, but always revealing. They show both the parts of yourself that are healed and those still seeking attention. They reflect your emotional strengths, vulnerabilities, patterns, and potential for growth. Healing within relationships is not about finding perfect people; it is about becoming emotionally aware enough to engage in connection in healthier, more grounded ways. This process involves recognizing old patterns, understanding your triggers, building emotional safety, setting boundaries, and holding yourself accountable with compassion.

As you evolve, your relationships will shift. Some will strengthen, others will fall away, and new ones will enter your life aligned with who you are becoming rather than who you used to be. This evolution is not loss; it is transformation. It is evidence that you are healing from the inside out. You deserve relationships that honor your voice, respect your boundaries, support your growth, and reflect the emerging version of yourself, not the version shaped by past pain.

This chapter invites you to look deeply into the mirror and ask yourself: What patterns are you ready to release, and what kinds of emotional connections are you ready to welcome?

Reflection Exercise: The Relationship Mirror

Take a few quiet moments to reflect or journal on the emotional patterns in your relationships and identify areas where you feel ready to grow. Consider how familiar dynamics have shaped your connections and what emotional safety truly looks like for you. Ask yourself where you struggle to set boundaries and notice how your triggers appear in your relationships today. Reflect on one relational pattern you are ready to break, and envision the healthier relationship experiences you are open to receiving. Write freely and honestly, your answers will serve as the blueprint for the healing explored in Chapter 4.

CHAPTER 4
The Power of Self-Recognition

Before healing can take root, before patterns can change, and before relationships can shift, something essential must happen: you must learn to recognize yourself. Not the version shaped by expectations. Not the version shaped by survival. Not the version shaped by pain. But the version that has quietly been waiting for permission to exist.

Self-recognition is the process of turning inward with honesty and courage. It means acknowledging the truths you've avoided, the emotions you've tucked away, and the strengths you've forgotten you possess. Healing begins here, in the intimate space where awareness meets acceptance.

Self-recognition also requires honesty with the reflections staring back at you. As we navigate life, it becomes easy to become married to other people's perspectives of us, their opinions, expectations, and unspoken standards. We begin performing for those who shape these ideas, molding ourselves into versions that make others comfortable while drifting further from who we truly are. Over time, these external definitions become internal beliefs, and we mistake them for identity. Genuine self-recognition, however, demands that we confront those reflections and ask a deeper question: Is this who I am, or who I learned to be? It calls us to continually remind ourselves of who we are and the path we desire to travel. Detours, setbacks, and pauses are negotiable, but the ultimate goal remains constant: to arrive at a destination of positive self-regard, where self-image is rooted in truth rather than perception, and authenticity rather than performance.

Many of us spend years disconnected from our true selves. Trauma, criticism, environmental instability, and unmet emotional needs can cause us to shapeshift into versions of ourselves designed to keep others comfortable while neglecting our own identity. Over time, we become skilled at performing instead of expressing, pleasing instead of asking, and surviving instead of living.

Self-recognition is your invitation to stop performing and start seeing. It challenges you to ask difficult questions: What beliefs about myself never belonged to me? What parts of me have I outgrown? What am I carrying that was never mine to hold? Who would I be without the weight of old stories? These questions shift your gaze inward and help reveal the truth beneath the conditioning.

Recognizing yourself is not an ego-driven pursuit, it is an act of emotional honesty. It calls you to look beyond your pain and see the full picture of who you are becoming. It requires confronting internal narratives formed during moments of fear, rejection, silence, or misunderstanding. It challenges you to separate the truth of who you are from the distortions created by past experiences.

The journey of self-recognition is both beautiful and uncomfortable. It illuminates strengths you forgot you had, exposes wounds you thought were healed, and challenges your beliefs, habits, and emotional autopilot. But it also frees you, because you cannot heal, evolve, or transform anything you refuse to acknowledge.

This chapter begins the work of coming home to yourself. Here, you will learn to identify the internal messages shaping your self-image, discern between your authentic voice and the inherited voices of your past, recognize the emotional signatures of wounded versus healed behavior, and begin crafting a new inner narrative grounded in truth rather than trauma.

Self-recognition isn't about perfection; it's about presence stepping fully into the awareness of who you are and who you are becoming. The clearer your inner vision grows, the more you will understand that healing doesn't begin with fixing it begins with seeing.

Distinguishing Between Your Voice and the Voices from Your Past

One of the most transformative aspects of self-recognition is learning to separate your authentic voice from the voices that were planted in you long before you understood their influence. The internal world is rarely silent; it often resembles an echo chamber filled with memories, teachings, criticisms, cultural messages, and the emotional atmospheres in which we were raised. Without awareness, these echoes can easily be mistaken for truth, shaping our choices and self-perception in ways we may not even notice.

The voices from our past are powerful because they were our earliest teachers, shaping our identity before we had the capacity to question or challenge what we were taught. Some of these voices nurtured strength, resilience, and determination. Others seeded fear, insecurity, silence, and self-doubt. These inherited messages often become the default soundtrack of our internal world, guiding our reactions and influencing our beliefs long after their original purpose has faded.

Most people don't realize how deeply these old voices affect their self-perception until they begin examining the stories they repeat internally. The real challenge lies in discerning what truly belongs to you, your beliefs, your values, your intuition versus what was imposed on you by upbringing, culture, emotional environments, or the unhealed individuals who shaped your early years.

Growing up as an African American female in a blended family of ten, the voices around me were loud, layered, and often difficult to distinguish. Our home environment was filled with constant noise: overlapping conversations, strong personalities, emotional expression, and the energetic rhythm that comes with a large household. Though such dynamics are common in big, blended families, there were many moments when I felt alone and disconnected. Not because I lacked people, but because emotional clarity often felt scarce in the crowded atmosphere. Amid that noise, I sensed early on that my calling was to become a therapist or counselor. Something inside me knew I was meant to understand people, hold space for emotions, and help others navigate their inner worlds the same terrain I often had to traverse on my own.

Yet, like many individuals walking toward their purpose, the voices from my past pushed back against that calling. They whispered reminders of my trauma, my struggles, and the idea that I couldn't possibly help others when I had endured so much myself. Those internalized doubts tried to convince me that my pain made me unqualified. But when I finally confronted those voices, questioning their truth and challenging their authority, I realized something profound: my trauma wasn't a disqualification; it was a credential. It equipped me with empathy, insight, understanding, and the ability to see beneath the surface of pain. It gave me the very tools I now use to help others.

This is the essence of distinguishing your voice from the voices of your past, recognizing that not every echo deserves your obedience. Some voices must be released. Others need to be reinterpreted. And some can be honored for the lessons they taught, even if they no longer define who you are becoming.

Your authentic voice is the one that calls you toward growth, healing, and possibility. It is steady and grounded. It challenges you without shaming you, pushes you without punishing you, and reflects your truth rather than your trauma. The voices from your past, however, often echo old fears, outdated beliefs, and limitations rooted in environments that no longer reflect your present reality.

Learning to reclaim your voice begins with pausing long enough to ask yourself:

Whose voice is speaking right now?

Is this truth or memory?

Is this intuition or fear?

Is this who I am, or who I have learned to be?

When you start recognizing these differences, something powerful shifts. You begin reclaiming the parts of yourself that were overshadowed by expectation. You stop internalizing beliefs that were never yours. You create space for your intuition to speak clearly, confidently, and consistently. Over time, your authentic voice grows stronger than the echoes of your past.

This is where emotional freedom begins, not by silencing your thoughts, but by learning which ones deserve your attention.

How Trauma Shapes Self-Perception

Trauma has a way of reshaping how we see ourselves long before we recognize its influence. It doesn't always enter our lives loudly; sometimes it arrives through subtle messages, emotional neglect, harsh criticism, or painful experiences that quietly teach us to question our value. Over time, trauma becomes a lens one that blurs the truth, magnifies our flaws, and distorts the way we interpret our abilities, relationships, and worth.

When we experience emotional disruption, especially at a young age, we internalize those moments as definitions. A single painful comment can become a belief. A repeated dismissal can become a script. A pattern of unpredictability can become a worldview. Trauma plants seeds of self-doubt that whisper: "You're not enough," "You're too much," "You're unworthy," or "You will never be anything other than what you've been told." These quiet messages linger because trauma trains the body and mind to anticipate pain, and this anticipation becomes part of how we see ourselves. Instead of viewing ourselves with clarity, we view ourselves through emotional residue.

Trauma can also lead us to assess ourselves unfairly, causing us to judge our identity through the harshness of what happened to us rather than the truth of who we are. There is a familiar saying: "Don't throw the baby out with the bathwater." This expression reminds us not to discard the fullness of our identity because of the parts shaped by pain. It creates space for resilience, redemption, and self-compassion to emerge when trauma tries to reinforce negative self-assessments. When trauma ambushes the picture you have of yourself, distorting judgment, activating old shame, or convincing you that your strengths don't matter, practice extending the same grace to yourself that you so freely offer to others. Grace interrupts the cycle of self-punishment, softens the impact of old wounds, and reminds you that healing is not invalidated by lingering hurt.

Trauma shapes self-perception by making the past feel present. A child who felt unheard may grow into an adult who apologizes before speaking. Someone who experienced emotional betrayal may struggle to trust their own intuition. A person raised in instability may learn to expect chaos even in calm environments. Trauma freezes emotional truths in time, making outdated fears feel current even when life has changed around us.

But the mind can learn and what it learned in trauma can be unlearned through healing. The first step is awareness: noticing when your self-perception is reacting to an old wound rather than present reality. The second step is discernment: recognizing the difference between your authentic voice and the voice of your trauma. The third step is reclamation: choosing not to relive an old narrative, but to rewrite it in a way that honors your growth.

Healing does not require erasing the past. It invites you to reinterpret it, to understand how it shaped you without allowing it to define you. Your trauma may be part of your story, but it is not the entirety of your identity. You are more than what hurt you, more than what you survived, and more than the fragmented beliefs you adopted while trying to cope.

As your self-perception begins to heal, you will notice subtle yet profound shifts. You may find yourself questioning old narratives instead of accepting them as truth. You may begin rediscovering strengths you thought were lost. You may see possibilities where fear once lived. Slowly, you begin to identify yourself not through the eyes of your trauma, but through the truth of who you are becoming.

This is the transformative power of healing your self-perception:

You emerge with a vision of yourself grounded not in wounds, but in wisdom not in fear, but in truth.

Rebuilding Your Inner Identity

As you begin separating your true voice from the echoes of your past and unraveling the distortions trauma created in your self-perception, you step into one of the most empowering phases of healing: rebuilding your inner identity. This is the stage where you no longer accept the old definitions handed to you and instead begin constructing a self-concept rooted in truth, strength, and authenticity. Rebuilding your identity is not about becoming someone new, it is about returning to who you were before the world taught you to shrink. Trauma may have interrupted your story, but it did not erase the core of who you are. Beneath the layers of fear, shame, doubt, and survival lies a self you may have forgotten but never lost.

This part of the journey requires intention. You must consciously decide which beliefs deserve to stay and which must go. It is emotional renovation, clearing out the inner debris that no longer serves you and strengthening the foundation on which your new sense of self will stand. Rebuilding your identity begins with acknowledging a vital truth: you get to decide who you are now. No one else gets to write that story, not your past, not your critics, not your trauma, and not the people who underestimated your ability to rise. You are no longer obligated to carry definitions shaped in pain.

This reconstruction process involves examining the "inner agreements" you've unconsciously lived by for years agreements such as "I am unworthy," "I must earn love," "My needs come last," or "I am too broken to become more." These are not truths; they are outdated contracts with your past. As you rebuild, you replace them with new agreements rooted in healing: "I deserve respect," "My voice matters," "I am capable of growth," "I am allowed to evolve," and "My past does not invalidate my purpose."

Rebuilding your identity also requires emotional courage the courage to stand firmly in who you are becoming, even when others expect the old version of you. It is the courage to say no where you once said yes out of fear. The courage to move forward even when familiar patterns try to pull you backward. And the courage to allow yourself to grow beyond the environments and relationships that once shaped you. It also means embracing the parts of yourself that trauma taught you to ignore, the creative part, the joyful part, the intuitive part, the confident part, the part that dared to dream before life taught you to doubt. Healing gives these pieces permission to return.

As you reclaim these parts, your internal landscape begins to shift. You feel more grounded, centered, and connected to yourself than you may have ever felt, or at least not since childhood. You stop filtering your identity through fear, judgment, or past experiences and begin defining yourself through clarity and intention. This is the moment you realize you are allowed to outgrow the version of yourself that trauma produced. You are allowed to redefine your worth. You are allowed to rewrite your narrative. You are allowed to evolve without apologizing for it.

Rebuilding your inner identity is not a single moment; it is a continuous practice of choosing to honor who you are becoming rather than who you were conditioned to be. With each step, you strengthen your foundation and reclaim your power. This is the rebirth, the reclaiming, the re-rooting of your soul in truth rather than trauma.

Reflective Exercise

Find a quiet space where you can sit with your thoughts without rush or interruption. Take a deep breath and allow your body to settle into the moment. This exercise is a gentle invitation to reconnect with the parts of yourself that trauma, criticism, and survival once overshadowed. As you reflect, write freely and honestly. There are no wrong answers, only truths waiting to be acknowledged.

Begin by considering the echoes of your past. Ask yourself which old messages, memories, or voices still influence how you see yourself today. Reflect on the phrases, beliefs, or emotional imprints that continue to follow you, even if you know they no longer fit who you are becoming. These internal echoes are important to identify because awareness is the first step in loosening their grip.

Next, turn inward and imagine the sound of your authentic voice, the voice beneath fear, shame, and old conditioning. What does this truest version of you want to say right now? What truth is it urging you to reclaim? Allow the words to rise without judgment, serving as reminders of who you are beneath everything you were taught to be.

Now, consider the narratives you are ready to release. Which aspects of your identity were shaped more by trauma than by truth? Identify at least one belief, fear, or internal storyline that no longer aligns with the person you are becoming. Naming it weakens its hold and creates space for healing.

As you rebuild your inner identity, notice which qualities and strengths are beginning to resurface. Which parts of your personality, calling, or dreams are returning now that you are making room for authenticity? These are the seeds of your evolving self, pieces that were buried but never lost.

From this place of clarity, create a new inner agreement. Write a declaration that honors your growth and shifts your internal narrative toward healing. It might sound like:

"I am learning to trust myself again."

"My story does not define my worth."

"I am allowed to become someone new."

"My voice matters, and I will no longer silence it."

Choose one truth that resonates deeply with you and commit it to memory. Let it become the foundation you carry into the next chapter of your healing journey.

Finally, take a moment to express gratitude for the path you are walking. Healing is not only about what you overcome, but also about who you become in the process. Write a brief reflection thanking yourself for the steps you've taken, the truths you've confronted, and the identity you are reclaiming. Acknowledge the courage it takes to rewrite your story from the inside out.

You are not returning to who you were before pain; you are becoming someone stronger, clearer, and more rooted in truth than ever before. Chapter 4 marks the beginning of that return, the moment you truly see yourself. And once you see yourself, you can never be lost again.

CHAPTER 5

The Healing Power of Self-Compassion: The Art of Emotional Nurturing

Healing is not a destination; it is a relationship, a relationship with yourself. By the time you reach this chapter, you have already begun the courageous work of self-recognition. You have challenged the old voices that once shaped your identity, revisited difficult memories, separated truth from distortion, and started rebuilding the foundation of who you are becoming. Now begins a new phase: learning how to care for the self you have reclaimed.

We often hear the phrase "give yourself grace," and in many ways, each of us can relate to how deeply this applies to our own stories. Grace is the origin of emotional nurturing. It softens the harsh edges of self-judgment, offers compassion where blame once lived, and provides the platform on which healing can take root. Grace is the meeting place between who you were and who you are becoming, a gentle reminder that your growth deserves patience, understanding, and care.

Emotional nurturing is the practice of tending to your inner world with the same tenderness, patience, and compassion that you so easily extend to others. It is an ongoing commitment to show up for yourself, not only in moments of strength and confidence but especially in moments of fear, uncertainty, or vulnerability. Emotional nurturing is where self-compassion becomes action.

Many of us were never taught how to care for ourselves emotionally. We learned how to survive, achieve, give, and endure, but not how to soothe our own fears, comfort our own pain, or validate our own feelings. Emotional nurturing fills this gap. It brings intention, warmth, and gentleness to the internal experiences we once ignored or criticized.

This practice is not about avoiding pain or pretending everything is okay. It is about creating an internal environment where all parts of you, the strong, the fragile, the fearful, the hopeful, feel safe to exist without judgment. Emotional nurturing says: "I will not abandon myself when I need support the most."

In this chapter, you will step into the art of caring for yourself by:

- Understanding the emotional needs that were overlooked or dismissed in the past
- Learning to self-soothe during moments of distress or overwhelm

- Responding to triggers with compassion rather than criticism
- Practicing emotional presence instead of emotional avoidance
- Building rituals of self-care that nourish your mind, body, and spirit
- Developing an inner dialogue rooted in kindness rather than condemnation

Emotional nurturing is the bridge between awareness and transformation. It allows healing to take root, turning insight into change, clarity into growth, and vulnerability into strength.

Perhaps most importantly, this chapter reveals a profound truth:

You don't have to wait for someone else to offer you what you've needed all along.

You can learn to give yourself comfort.

You can learn to create emotional safety from within.

You can learn to be present for yourself in ways no one ever was for you.

At the heart of emotional nurturing lies this truth:

You deserve care that is consistent, compassionate, and unwavering from others, yes, but especially from yourself.

As we move deeper into this chapter, you will explore what emotional nurturing looks like in daily practice, why it may feel unfamiliar at first, and how it can become one of the most powerful tools for long-term healing.

You have learned to see yourself.

Now, you will learn to hold yourself.

The Role of Acknowledgment in Emotional Nurturing

Emotional nurturing begins with acknowledgment the simple yet profound act of recognizing what is true within you. Acknowledgment can be defined as the acceptance of the truth or existence of something, whether it is an emotion, a memory, a need, or a wound. When we refuse to acknowledge our internal reality, we unintentionally create emotional distress, because what we do not name, we cannot process, and what we cannot process continues to influence us in ways we may not understand. Often, it is the lack of acknowledgment that generates the deepest discomfort, the tension that arises when something inside us demands attention, yet we keep trying to silence it.

Acknowledgment is the first step of emotional nurturing because it invites honesty without judgment. It allows you to say, "This is how I feel," "This is what I'm carrying," "This is what hurt me," "This is what I need," without minimizing or dismissing your own experience. For many people, acknowledgment feels foreign because they were taught to ignore their emotions, minimize their pain, or "push through" discomfort without ever pausing to understand it. But nurturing cannot occur in the dark. Healing requires light and acknowledgment is the switch that turns it on.

When you acknowledge your truth, you create space for emotional clarity. You remove the pressure of pretending, performing, or suppressing. You grant yourself permission to be human. In doing so, you also reduce the intensity of emotional overwhelm. A feeling acknowledged is a feeling that begins to soften. A wound acknowledged is a wound on its way to healing. A need acknowledged is a need that can finally be met.

Acknowledgment also nurtures self-compassion. When you allow your emotions to exist without resistance, you send a powerful internal message:

"I am worth understanding. My feelings matter. My experiences are valid."

This kind of emotional validation forms the foundation of inner safety, the safety that allows all parts of you to be seen, heard, and cared for.

Emotional nurturing cannot happen without acknowledgment because nurturing requires presence. You cannot soothe what you refuse to face. You cannot comfort what you are unwilling to name. You cannot heal what you pretend does not exist. Acknowledgment brings the truth forward so that healing can finally begin.

In the chapters leading here, you have learned to recognize your voice, separate it from the echoes of your past, and understand how trauma shaped your self-perception. Now, acknowledgment becomes the bridge between awareness and nurturing the tender moment when you pause long enough to say:

"This is where I am, and I am willing to care for myself here."

Understanding Emotional Needs

One of the most overlooked aspects of healing is recognizing that emotional needs are not weaknesses, they are an essential part of being human. Every person, regardless of background, upbringing, or personality, carries a set of emotional needs that shape how they feel, connect, and function in the world. Yet many of us were never taught how to identify these needs, much less how to honor them.

Instead, we were taught to "be strong," "push through," "not make a fuss," or "keep it together." Over time, these messages encouraged us to disconnect from the very signals designed to guide our emotional health. When emotional needs go unacknowledged, they do not disappear, they simply find new ways to express themselves. This can manifest as irritability, anxiety, shutdown, resentment, exhaustion, or even physical symptoms without explanation.

Understanding your emotional needs is a foundational step in emotional nurturing because you cannot tend a garden you refuse to see. Your emotional needs are internal indicators that tell you when something is missing, overwhelming, or asking for care. They are not burdens; they are invitations.

Some emotional needs are universal, the need for safety, acceptance, belonging, respect, and compassion. Others are shaped by your personality, experiences, and history. For those who grew up in environments where emotional expression was dismissed, chaotic, or unsafe, learning to understand emotional needs may feel confusing or unfamiliar. It may even stir guilt or discomfort, especially if you were taught that your needs were excessive, inconvenient, or insignificant.

But emotional needs do not make you "too much." They make you human.

Understanding your emotional needs means becoming curious about your internal responses rather than judging them. It requires noticing moments when you feel unseen, unheard, overwhelmed, or emotionally empty, not to criticize yourself, but to understand what unmet need is signaling for attention.

Sometimes the need is for reassurance, clarity, or connection.

Sometimes it is for solitude, rest, or boundaries.

Sometimes it is for kindness, patience, or emotional safety.

And sometimes it is for healing the younger parts of you that never received the nurturing they deserved.

As you explore your emotional needs, you may discover that many were shaped by experiences of neglect, trauma, or emotional inconsistency. A child who was not comforted learns to silence fear. A teen who was criticized learns to suppress vulnerability. An adult who was unsupported learns to avoid asking for help. But beneath these survival strategies, the original needs remain, waiting to be acknowledged.

Emotional nurturing becomes possible when you allow yourself to accept that your needs are valid. Not excessive. Not dramatic. Not inconvenient. Valid.

When you give your emotional needs permission to exist, you begin to build an inner world where healing can flourish. You begin responding to yourself with care instead of criticism. You begin understanding your triggers rather than shaming yourself for them. You begin allowing your emotions to speak without immediately silencing them.

Understanding your emotional needs begins with listening to yourself with compassion.

It involves honoring the parts of you that are still learning to trust your own care.

It means recognizing that your needs are not a problem they are a roadmap.

As you learn to follow that map, you will uncover a truth many people never realize:

Your emotional needs were never too much; they were simply too often unmet.

Learning to Self-Soothe

Self-soothing is one of the most powerful emotional tools you can develop, yet for many, it remains unfamiliar. If you were not taught emotional comfort in childhood, if your feelings were dismissed, minimized, punished, or overlooked, calming your own distress as an adult can feel confusing, even impossible. But the ability to soothe yourself is not innate; it is a skill you learn, practice, and strengthen over time.

Self-soothing is the intentional act of grounding your emotions when they feel overwhelming. It is the practice of reminding your body and mind that you are safe, present, and capable of handling the moment. When we self-soothe, we communicate internally: I am here for you. You are not alone. We can get through this together.

Many people confuse self-soothing with avoidance, but the two could not be more different. Avoidance pushes emotions away; self-soothing acknowledges them while gently regulating their intensity. Avoidance numbs, self-soothing nurtures. Avoidance delays healing; self-soothing supports it.

Learning to self-soothe begins with awareness, noticing the signs of emotional activation. Perhaps your breathing becomes shallow, your chest tightens, your thoughts race, or your stomach knots. These are signals from your body saying, "I feel unsafe." When you respond with self-soothing instead of panic or judgment, you teach your body a new truth: We don't have to relive the past. We can choose calm.

Effective self-soothing engages both the mind and the body. It can include slowing your breathing until your heartbeat steadies, placing your hand over your heart to anchor your nervous system, or grounding yourself by focusing on the sensations around you, the temperature of the air, the texture beneath your feet, the rhythm of your breath. Sometimes self-soothing means speaking to yourself with compassion, offering the words you needed to hear long ago: You're safe. You're doing your best. This feeling will pass. You have survived worse than this.

Self-soothing can also involve physical acts that bring comfort wrapping yourself in a blanket, taking a warm shower, stepping outside for fresh air, journaling your emotions, listening to calming music, or engaging in gentle movement like stretching or walking. These small gestures send a powerful message to your nervous system: I am nurturing you.

Over time, self-soothing becomes a form of emotional reparenting, giving yourself the comfort, validation, and calm that you may not have consistently received growing up. It allows you to become a stable emotional presence in your own life, teaches your mind to trust your ability to cope, and helps you move through distress without collapsing into old patterns or reacting from past wounds.

The more you practice self-soothing, the more emotionally resilient you become. Distressing moments feel less overwhelming because you know you have the inner tools to manage them. Triggers lose some of their intensity as your body learns a new response. Emotional waves no longer drown you; instead, you learn to ride them with steadiness and grace.

Self-soothing is not a weakness; it is a strength. It is the ultimate expression of emotional maturity, the art of being your own anchor when life becomes stormy. It is a reminder that healing is not about eliminating pain but about learning to respond to it differently.

As you strengthen this skill, you will find yourself becoming calmer, clearer, and more in control of your internal world. You will no longer fear your emotions; instead, you will understand them. And in that understanding, you will discover something transformative:

You are capable of giving yourself the safety you once believed only others could provide.

Responding to Triggers with Compassion

Triggers are not signs of weakness; they are signals of unresolved pain seeking attention. When something in the present awakens a past wound, the emotional reaction can feel sudden, overwhelming, or even disproportionate to the situation. For many of us, the instinct is to judge ourselves for feeling "too much," to shut down to avoid discomfort, or to push past the feeling as quickly as possible. True healing, however, requires a gentler approach: meeting your triggered self with compassion rather than criticism.

A trigger is not the enemy; it is information. It shows where your heart is still tender, reveals the parts of you that haven't felt safe in a long time, and uncovers emotional truths beneath the surface, truths that need gentleness, not judgment. Responding with compassion begins with awareness. Instead of reacting automatically or slipping into self-blame, you pause long enough to acknowledge what is happening within you. In that pause, you create emotional space, a breath between the past and the present, where you allow yourself to feel without being consumed by the feeling.

Compassion in these moments sounds like understanding rather than reprimand. It may sound like, "This reaction makes sense based on what I've lived through," or "I am safe in this moment, even if my body remembers something painful." It may also sound like permission: "It's okay to slow down and take care of myself right now," or "I don't need to be ashamed of having emotions." When you respond this way, you interrupt the cycle of self-punishment. Instead of criticizing yourself for being reactive or overwhelmed, you recognize the bravery it takes to confront emotional pain. You begin to understand that a trigger is not a flaw it is an opportunity for insight.

Compassion also includes tending to your emotional needs in real time. This might mean grounding yourself through deep breathing, stepping away from a stressful environment, placing a hand over your heart to soothe your nervous system, or speaking to yourself with the same tenderness you would offer a hurting child. Self-soothing is not self-indulgence; it is stabilization. It reassures your body that the danger has passed and affirms that you are capable of providing the emotional safety you once lacked.

It is important to remember that triggers often stem from moments in your past when you felt unheard, unprotected, or invalidated. By responding with compassion now, you offer yourself what you never received then. Over time, this practice rewires your emotional responses. The more consistently you meet your pain with understanding, the less power your triggers hold over your life. You begin to remain grounded in the present without collapsing into old narratives. You learn to process emotions as they arise instead of reliving past wounds.

Responding to triggers with compassion is not about eliminating discomfort, it is about transforming your relationship with it. It shifts your focus from shame to understanding, from fear to curiosity, and from emotional survival to emotional healing. This is one of the most sacred forms of emotional nurturing: the ability to hold yourself gently in the moments when your history meets your present.

Practicing Emotional Presence

Emotional presence is the commitment to stay with yourself, your thoughts, your feelings, your sensations without running, numbing, or disconnecting. It is one of the deepest forms of emotional nurturing because it teaches you that you do not have to abandon yourself when things become uncomfortable. Many of us learned early on to cope with pain by distancing ourselves from it: pushing feelings aside, pretending we are fine, distracting ourselves with work or caretaking, or shrinking our emotional needs to avoid being a burden. While these strategies may have helped us survive, they create emotional distance that prevents true healing.

Practicing emotional presence means gently reversing that pattern. It invites you to turn toward your internal experience with curiosity rather than avoidance. Instead of silencing your feelings, you allow them to speak. Instead of rushing past discomfort, you give yourself permission to pause. You acknowledge what is happening in your inner world without judgment, allowing emotions to rise and fall naturally. Emotional presence does not demand that you "fix" anything, only that you be willing to notice what is true in the moment.

Being emotionally present often begins with small acts of awareness. It might look something like noticing tightness in your chest and asking yourself which emotion it is connected to. It may involve identifying a sense of irritation or sadness and allowing yourself to feel it rather than masking it with productivity or dismissal. It may be as simple as placing a hand over your heart and saying, "I'm here with you," when you feel overwhelmed. These are quiet moments of self-partnership, moments that teach your mind and body that your emotions are not threats, but messages.

Practicing emotional presence also means resisting the urge to judge or shame yourself for how you feel. Instead of labeling emotions as "overreactions," "weakness," or "too much," you begin to understand them as valid expressions of your inner experience. When you honor your emotional truth without minimizing it, you build trust with yourself. You create an inner environment where honesty is safe and authenticity is welcome.

Over time, emotional presence strengthens your ability to remain grounded even in difficult moments. It allows you to experience emotions fully without being consumed by them. You begin to respond to your internal world with stability and clarity rather than panic or avoidance. This presence makes healing possible because you cannot transform what you refuse to acknowledge.

Practicing emotional presence is not about being emotionally perfect, it is about being emotionally available. It is an act of compassion, patience, and courage, teaching you that you deserve to be witnessed, supported, and understood, especially by yourself. As you continue to embrace emotional presence, you will find that this simple commitment becomes one of the most transformative parts of your healing journey, allowing you to show up in your life with authenticity, depth, and resilience.

Building Rituals of Self-Care

Self-care is often misunderstood as an occasional treat or a luxury reserved for moments of rest, but true self-care is far deeper and far more consistent. It is the intentional practice of tending to your emotional, mental, and physical well-being in ways that sustain you, not just soothe you temporarily. Emotional maintenance is intentional, and self-care runs parallel to that maintenance, it is the ongoing commitment to keep your inner world aligned, nourished, and supported.

Many people associate self-care with financial costs, elaborate routines, or the need for extended free time. However, genuine self-care does not depend on money, elaborate experiences, or even long stretches of solitude. It can be as simple as practicing mindfulness, pausing to breathe, or engaging in grounding techniques that help you remain present and regulated in your daily life. Self-care is not limited to days off, vacations, or quiet weekends; it can happen in the middle of your workday, during a stressful moment, or while navigating everyday responsibilities. It exists in the choices you make, moment by moment, to support your emotional balance and honor your internal needs.

Building rituals of self-care means creating practices that you return to consistently, rituals that anchor you, soothe you, and bring you back into alignment when life becomes overwhelming. These rituals may include journaling to release emotional tension, meditating to center your thoughts, stretching or walking to reconnect with your body, speaking affirmations that strengthen your inner dialogue, or simply sitting still long enough to check in with yourself. The power of self-care lies not in its complexity but in its intention. Every small act of care reinforces the message: I am worthy of my own attention.

When self-care becomes a ritual rather than an afterthought, it begins to reshape your emotional landscape. You become more attuned to your needs, more grounded in your responses, and more resilient during moments of stress. You learn to show up for yourself not only when life is calm, but especially when life is challenging. In this way, self-care becomes a form of emotional nurturing, a steady reminder that you deserve consistency, compassion, and intentional care from the person you rely on most: yourself.

Holding Yourself With Grace

As you reach the end of this chapter, you have stepped into one of the most tender and transformative parts of healing: learning to care for yourself with intention. Emotional nurturing is not a single act but a continuous relationship that evolves as you evolve. You have begun to understand your emotional needs, soothe yourself through moments of overwhelm, respond gently to your triggers, and build rituals that honor your well-being. These practices are more than coping strategies; they are expressions of self-respect.

You have also learned that giving yourself grace is not a cliché; it is the foundation of emotional restoration. Grace softens the inner critic. Grace allows you to embrace the parts of yourself that are still learning and growing. Grace creates room for imperfection while reminding you that you are worthy of care, tenderness, and patience.

As you deepen your commitment to emotional nurturing, you will begin to notice subtle yet profound shifts within yourself. You may find that you speak to yourself kindlier, recover more quickly after emotional setbacks, and no longer abandon yourself in moments of vulnerability. You begin to trust that you can hold yourself not perfectly, but consistently, and that trust becomes one of the strongest pillars of your healing.

This chapter is not the end of your emotional nurturing journey; it is the beginning of a lifelong practice: a practice where you choose compassion over criticism, presence over avoidance, and care over neglect, a practice where you honor your emotional landscape with the same tenderness you longed for from others.

As you move forward, remember this truth:

You are both the healer and the one being healed.

You are the nurturer and the one who needs nurture.

You are the safe space you have been waiting for.

Reflection Exercise: The Heart of Emotional Nurturing

Find a quiet moment to breathe deeply and center your spirit. Approach these questions with openness, honesty, and compassion. Your reflections will help reinforce the emotional nurturing practices introduced in this chapter.

1. How Do I Offer Myself Grace?

Take a moment to reflect on the last time you judged yourself harshly.

How might you have approached that situation with greater kindness and understanding?

What would it have looked like to truly give yourself grace in that moment?

2. What Emotional Needs Am I Now Aware Of?

Reflect on the emotional needs that were overlooked, dismissed, or misunderstood in the past.

Which of these needs are you becoming more aware of and attentive to today?

3. How Do I Care for Myself When I'm Overwhelmed?

Consider the grounding techniques or self-soothing strategies that help you feel safe.

Which practices bring you back to emotional balance?

4. What Triggers Am I Learning to Meet With Compassion?

Identify a trigger that you encountered recently.

How did you respond?

How might compassion have changed the experience?

5. What Rituals Support My Emotional Well-Being?

Reflect on the daily or weekly practices that help you nurture your inner world.

Are there new rituals you want to begin?

Which one feels most grounding?

6. What New Commitment Am I Making to Myself?

Write a short statement affirming the kind of emotional care you will offer yourself moving forward. This might sound like:

- *I will listen to my emotions without judgment.*
- *I will honor my limits without guilt.*
- *I will nurture myself with consistency and compassion.*

Closing Thought

As you continue your healing journey, remember that emotional nurturing is not about perfection, it is about presence. It is about returning to yourself, repeatedly, especially on the days when compassion feels hardest to give. With every act of self-care, you strengthen your relationship with yourself and build a foundation of emotional safety that no one can take away.

You have learned to recognize yourself.

You have learned to hold yourself.

And because of this, you will never move through your healing journey alone.

CHAPTER 6
Becoming the Architect of Your Healing

Healing does not happen by accident. It is built by choice moment by moment, awareness by awareness. By the time you arrive at this chapter, you have learned to see yourself more clearly, to care for yourself more gently, and to treat your inner world with the tenderness it deserves. Now, you step into a new phase of growth: becoming intentional about the life you are creating moving forward.

There comes a point in every healing journey where awareness is no longer enough. You begin to sense a shift, a quiet, steady call toward transformation. You realize that while your past shaped you, it can no longer be allowed to lead you. Your identity is no longer defined by survival but guided by conscious choice. This is the moment when healing deepens into reconstruction.

Chapter 6 is about agency, reclaiming the power to direct your emotional, spiritual, and relational evolution. It is about stepping into the role of architect and shaping both the internal and external environments that support the person you are becoming. Healing asks you not only to release what wounded you but also to intentionally build what strengthens you.

While many begin their healing journey focused on what they want to change, true transformation comes from deciding what they want to create. You are not here merely to dismantle old patterns; you are here to design new ones, patterns rooted in clarity rather than confusion, alignment rather than reaction, authenticity rather than performance, and purpose rather than pain.

This chapter introduces you to the next dimension of healing: choosing alignment instead of obligation, designing emotional habits that reinforce growth, creating internal structure through values, boundaries, and spiritual grounding, cultivating environments and relationships that honor your evolution, and learning to live from intention rather than old narratives.

This is where healing becomes leadership the leadership of your own life. You are no longer simply responding to circumstances; you are shaping the conditions that allow you to thrive. You begin to trust your voice, honor your capacity, and build a life that reflects your truth rather than your trauma. Healing has escorted you back home to yourself. Chapter 6 teaches you how to live from that home with purpose, alignment, and emotional autonomy.

Choosing Alignment Over Survival Mode

Survival mode teaches you how to get through life, but alignment teaches you how to truly live it. For many, the instinct to survive became a way of being long before language existed to describe it. Survival mode is reactive, it responds to threat, instability, pressure, or emotional unpredictability. It sharpens vigilance, accelerates decision-making, and creates a sense of urgency that keeps the body and mind in constant motion. While survival mode may have protected you once, it cannot guide you toward the life you truly want to build.

Alignment, on the other hand, is intentional. It is the conscious choice to live in harmony with your values, your emotional truth, your spiritual grounding, and the life you feel called to create. Alignment shifts you from reacting to life to leading it. It is the moment you decide that your inner world deserves consistency, honesty, clarity, and peace.

But alignment requires discipline. It calls for honesty with yourself about the patterns that no longer serve you, the habits that drain you, and the environments that keep you small. Fear-driven responses, particularly the fight, flight, or freeze patterns, often become barriers to alignment because they are rooted in avoidance, urgency, and emotional protection. These reactions make it difficult to sit still long enough to assess what you truly need. They convince you to keep moving, keep pleasing, keep performing, rather than slowing down and confronting your inner truth.

Alignment removes these barriers by restoring balance. It invites you to listen inwardly instead of reacting outwardly. It teaches you to move from clarity rather than fear. And just like a vehicle with an unaligned tire, the signs of misalignment are impossible to ignore. When even one area of your life wobbles, emotionally, spiritually, mentally, or relationally, the imbalance touches everything. The ride becomes unsteady, and the sense of unease follows you into every part of your day. Only when you stop, assess the issue, and commit to making the necessary adjustments do comfort, stability, and direction return.

Choosing alignment means noticing the wobble instead of pretending it isn't there. It means addressing discomfort rather than adapting to it. It means choosing long-term peace over short-term coping. When you consciously shift out of survival mode and into alignment, you give yourself permission to make decisions from wisdom instead of fear, intention instead of impulsiveness, and emotional clarity instead of inherited patterns.

Alignment is not a one-time decision; it is a continuous commitment to returning to yourself, repeatedly, until your inner life supports the outer life you are building. It is the pathway to emotional autonomy, spiritual grounding, and the stable foundation your healing journey has been preparing you for.

Designing Emotional Habits That Reinforce Growth

Growth is not the product of occasional breakthroughs; it is the result of consistent emotional habits practiced over time. Emotional habits are the small, daily choices that shape how you think, respond, communicate, and care for yourself. They are the internal behaviors that determine whether you remain anchored in your healing or drift back into old patterns rooted in survival.

Designing emotional habits requires intention. It invites you to examine the moments that typically pull you off center, moments when you shut down, overextend yourself, silence your needs, or slip into self-criticism, and intentionally replace those reflexes with practices that support your evolution. These habits become the emotional architecture of your new life, reinforcing the alignment you are learning to choose each day.

Instead of reacting impulsively, you begin responding thoughtfully.

Instead of internalizing everything, you begin expressing with clarity.

Instead of ignoring your needs, you begin honoring them.

Instead of operating from fear, you begin moving from grounded awareness.

Emotional habits are powerful not because they are dramatic, but because they are consistent. They train your mind and body to choose stability over chaos, truth over panic, presence over avoidance, and compassion over judgment. Each small shift, pausing before reacting, naming what you feel, taking a deep breath, choosing a boundary, extending grace to yourself, becomes a brick in the foundation of a healthier emotional life.

Intentional emotional habits might look like:

Checking in with your feelings before checking in with the world.

Setting limits on conversations or environments that drain your spirit.

Honoring your body's signals instead of pushing through exhaustion or discomfort.

Journaling to process emotions rather than suppressing them.

Practicing mindfulness or grounding when anxiety begins to rise.

Speaking to yourself with kindness rather than condemnation.

Allowing yourself to rest without guilt.

Communicating your needs instead of assuming they won't be met.

Celebrating small wins rather than waiting for perfection.

These habits will not always feel natural at first, especially if you were conditioned to prioritize others, live in survival mode, or minimize your emotional needs. But over time, repetition becomes reinforcement. Each day you choose healing; the path becomes easier to walk. Your emotional habits begin to replace the unhealthy patterns you once relied on, creating a new default: one rooted in self-awareness, self-respect, and emotional stability.

Designing emotional habits is ultimately an act of self-leadership. It declares:

I am no longer waiting for life to shape me; I am shaping the life I want to live.

It is the practice of showing up for yourself consistently, not just in moments of crisis. It is the commitment to nurture your growth even on days when you feel tired or discouraged. And it is the acknowledgment that healing is not defined by how perfectly you move forward, but by how intentionally you choose to rise each time you slip.

Growth becomes real when it becomes a habit.

And habits become powerful when they become a way of being.

Creating Internal Structure Through Values, Boundaries, and Spiritual Grounding

Healing becomes sustainable when you build an internal structure strong enough to support the person you are becoming. Awareness alone cannot hold your growth; it needs a framework. Without structure, healing is inconsistent, easily shaken by stress, emotions, or old patterns. But when you anchor yourself in clear values, firm boundaries, and spiritual grounding, you create a stable foundation that sustains your transformation even in difficult seasons.

Internal structure is not about rigidity; it is about alignment. It is the intentional process of deciding what matters to you, what guides you, and what you will no longer compromise. This structure keeps you steady when emotions fluctuate, when relationships shift, and when life presents challenges that once would have pulled you back into survival mode.

Values act as your internal compass. They help you make decisions rooted in purpose rather than fear, clarity rather than confusion, and authenticity rather than pressure. When you know your values, peace, integrity, compassion, spiritual alignment, growth, honesty, emotional safety, you navigate life with greater confidence. You stop reacting impulsively and begin choosing intentionally. You stop living according to external expectations and start living from internal truth.

Your values tell you:

"This is who I am."

"This is how I move through the world."

"This is what I refuse to sacrifice."

Boundaries reinforce those values. Values name what matters to you; boundaries protect it. They shape how you allow others to treat you, how you treat yourself, and how you maintain emotional balance. Boundaries create the space you need to live according to the standards you have set, not the demands others impose. Without boundaries, values remain theoretical; with boundaries, they become lived reality.

Spiritual grounding completes the structure by offering stability beyond circumstances. It provides meaning, direction, and connection to something greater than your fears or limitations. Spiritual grounding can include faith practices, meditation, prayer, reflection, nature, or anything that connects you to a higher purpose. This grounding reminds you that you are not navigating life alone, that your healing has guidance, support, and intention behind it.

When values, boundaries, and spiritual grounding work together, your internal world becomes anchored. You no longer bend to every emotional gust or external pressure. You no longer shrink when old triggers arise. You no longer lose yourself in relationships, obligations, or the noise of life.

This internal structure helps you:

- Stay aligned even when emotions spike

- Remain grounded during conflict or stress
- Make decisions that honor your growth
- Protect your energy from emotional drain
- Stay connected to purpose and spiritual direction
- Maintain clarity when old patterns tempt you back

You begin to experience emotional steadiness, a sense of inner balance that feels unfamiliar at first yet grows deeply empowering over time. The more you anchor your healing in values, boundaries, and spiritual grounding, the more your life starts to reflect the person you are becoming, rather than the person you were once forced to be.

Healing becomes not just something you feel, it becomes something you actively build.

Cultivating Environments That Support Your Evolution

Healing cannot thrive in environments that constantly trigger your wounds. True growth requires space, emotionally, mentally, and sometimes physically, where you feel grounded enough to expand. As you step into the intentional phase of your healing journey, one truth becomes clear:

Your environment is not neutral. It is either nurturing your evolution or stalling it.

For many of us, environments were something we simply adjusted to. We learned to adapt, to tolerate, to endure. We shaped ourselves around chaotic households, emotionally unpredictable relationships, or workplaces and communities that demanded survival rather than authenticity. But as healing deepens, adaptation is no longer the goal, alignment is. You begin to understand that the spaces you inhabit should reflect the person you are becoming, not the patterns you are trying to outgrow.

Cultivating a supportive environment starts with examining the energies, influences, and atmospheres you allow into your life. Ask yourself: Does this space calm me or drain me? Does this relationship strengthen me or diminish me? Does this routine bring clarity or chaos? Does this environment allow me to breathe, or does it require me to shrink? These questions help illuminate where emotional pruning may be necessary.

A supportive environment is not defined solely by silence, peace, or absence of conflict. It is defined by emotional safety, where your needs are respected, your truth is welcomed, and your presence is not negotiated. It is a space where your values are mirrored, your boundaries are honored, and your growth is encouraged rather than envied or dismissed.

Sometimes cultivating a healthy environment requires creating new spaces, the quiet corner where you journal, the spiritual or therapeutic community where you feel seen, the friendships where mutual growth is honored, the routines that regulate your nervous system. Other times, it requires gracefully stepping away from environments that keep you bound to older versions of yourself.

As you heal, you will notice your tolerance for chaos decreases. This is not weakness; it is wisdom. It is your spirit recognizing that unfamiliar peace is healthier than familiar dysfunction. You begin to crave environments that match the internal grounding you are cultivating: spaces that feel intentional, relationships that feel reciprocal, and lifestyles that reflect emotional maturity.

Cultivating supportive environments also means tending to the environment within yourself. Your internal landscape, your thoughts, inner dialogue, spiritual practices, emotional boundaries, becomes the foundation on which every external environment rests. When your inner world is structured by clarity, compassion, and alignment, the outer world begins to organize itself around that stability.

And as you continue to choose environments that honor your healing, something powerful happens:

You stop surviving in spaces that were never meant for you and start thriving in spaces designed with your evolution in mind. You begin to recognize that you are worthy of peace, of respect, of belonging, and of environments that nourish rather than drain your becoming.

Cultivating supportive environments is not a luxury; it is a requirement for sustained healing. It is the soil where your transformation can take root, grow, and flourish.

Living With Intention Rather Than Old Narratives

Living from intention means choosing to lead your life rather than letting old narratives, past conditioning, or inherited beliefs steer it for you. It is the shift from operating on emotional autopilot to consciously deciding how you think, respond, and move through the world. When you live intentionally, you no longer allow wounded identities to dictate your choices. Instead, you anchor yourself in clarity, purpose, and self-defined truth.

This shift is not passive, it requires a deliberate, ongoing commitment to rise above the stories that once confined you. For many of us, the narratives handed to us in childhood were rooted in someone else's pain, limitations, or inability to see our potential. And because those narratives came from people we trusted or depended on, they often felt like truth.

I remember being told by a parental figure that I would never be anything, never achieve anything, and never find success. Those words were meant to diminish me, to confine me, to shape a future that mirrored their limited understanding of who I was. But instead of letting that narrative define me, I chose to confront it. I chose to rise above it. I decided to challenge that statement rather than seek approval from the one who spoke it. That decision, that moment of choosing my own truth over someone else's projection, became the catalyst for who I am today and who I continue to become.

This is what it means to live with intention: refusing to let the wounds of your past narrate your future. It means choosing beliefs that empower you, behaviors that align with your purpose, and environments that honor your growth. It means acting from self-awareness rather than fear, from clarity rather than confusion, and from authenticity rather than performance.

Living intentionally also requires courage, the courage to evaluate your life honestly, disrupt patterns that no longer serve you, and release identities formed in survival rather than in truth. It calls you to create meaning rather than seek permission, to build your path rather than wait for one to appear, and to trust your vision even when others cannot see it.

The more you choose intention over old narratives, the more your life begins to align with who you truly are, rather than who you were told to be. You begin to recognize your capacity, honor your worth, and step into the fullness of your potential without apology. Slowly, your life transforms, not because the past disappears, but because it no longer dictates your direction.

This is the heart of intentional living:

You reclaim authorship.

You reclaim direction.

You reclaim identity.

And you step boldly into the life you were meant to live, not the one you were conditioned to accept.

Embodying Your Transformation

There comes a point in the healing journey when insight is no longer something you simply understand, it becomes something you live. Embodiment is the stage where the lessons you have learned begin to shape your posture, your decisions, your boundaries, your relationships, and your daily rhythm. It is the moment when healing stops being an internal process and becomes a visible expression of who you are becoming.

Embodying your transformation means stepping fully into the identity you have worked so hard to reclaim. It means no longer shrinking to fit old narratives or contorting yourself to meet outdated expectations. It means walking with the quiet confidence that comes from knowing you have survived, healed, and evolved, not by accident, but by intention.

This stage requires courage. Living from your healed self will challenge the dynamics that once relied on your wounded self. People who benefited from your silence may struggle with your voice. Environments that once felt familiar may now feel constricting. Patterns that once provided comfort may begin to feel misaligned. Embodiment asks you to honor these shifts instead of resisting them.

You begin making decisions that reflect your values rather than your fears.

You align your choices with your purpose rather than your past.

You choose peace even when chaos is familiar.

You honor your limits instead of overriding them for approval.

You trust your intuition because you have learned to distinguish it from trauma.

Embodying your transformation also means embracing the version of yourself that once felt out of reach. You allow yourself to take up space, pursue your dreams, accept opportunities, and believe that abundance is possible for you. You stop negotiating your worth. You stop returning to places where you had to beg for understanding. You stop apologizing for being who you were always meant to be.

This is where healing meets identity.

This is where authenticity replaces survival.

This is where you begin living from your power rather than your pain.

Embodying your transformation is not about perfection, it is about consistency. It is the ongoing choice to honor the person you have become, even on days when doubt whispers or old habits tug at your sleeve. The difference now is that you have the tools, awareness, and inner structure to return to alignment.

Most importantly, embodiment is a declaration:

"I am no longer living in the shadow of who I used to be."

You are living from your truth.

You are living from your healing.

You are living from intention.

And that choice becomes the foundation for everything you build next.

As you reach the end of this chapter, pause and acknowledge the transformation already unfolding within you. You have moved beyond awareness and into intentional creation, a shift that marks the transition from healing your past to building your future. Healing has taught you to recognize yourself, nurture yourself, and free yourself from old narratives; now you are learning to lead yourself with clarity, alignment, and purpose. This chapter invites you to sit with the identity you are actively constructing and reflect on the life you are choosing to design.

Find a quiet moment to breathe deeply and settle into your inner world. Allow your thoughts to gather naturally, without judgment or pressure. This reflection is not about finding the "right" answers; it is about meeting yourself honestly, exactly where you are.

Consider the ways you have begun choosing alignment over mere survival. Reflect on moments when you replaced patterns of urgency, fear, or emotional autopilot with intentional action. Ask yourself where alignment still feels difficult and what emotional barriers, such as fear, avoidance, or self-doubt, are requesting your attention. Notice the strength it takes to choose discipline over comfort, and truth over familiarity.

Next, think about the emotional habits you are forming. Which habits support the future you are building, and which reflect an older version of yourself? Sit with the awareness of how small choices shape your emotional landscape. Growth is rarely loud; it unfolds in the quiet decisions you make every day.

Reflect on the internal structures you are creating, your values, boundaries, and the principles guiding your choices. How are these structures supporting your emotional stability? Where might they need reinforcement? Notice how grounding yourself in what matters most allows you to navigate life with greater clarity and confidence.

Gently turn your attention to the environments and relationships you are cultivating. What spaces make you feel expansive, supported, and safe? What environments constrict your growth or pull you back into patterns you have outgrown? Take a moment to honor the spaces you have left behind, and the courage it required to do so.

Finally, reflect on what it means to live your truth. Healing has opened the door for you to move through life with authenticity rather than seeking approval, with intention rather than reaction. Consider the bold decisions you have made, like rising above the voice that once told you that you would never be anything and recognize how each moment of defiance became a steppingstone toward your purpose. These decisions were not random; they were declarations of who you are and who you are becoming.

Close this reflection by acknowledging your own leadership. You are no longer living from the remnants of who you were, you are living from the clarity of who you choose to be. Honor your resilience, your discipline, your alignment, and your truth. You are creating a life rooted not in trauma, but in intentionality, vision, and emotional autonomy.

Chapter 6 leaves you with this reminder:

Healing brought you home. Intention will teach you how to live there.

CHAPTER 7
Integrating The New Self

Healing is not simply about who you were or who you are becoming, it is about learning to live as the person you have worked so hard to reclaim. Transformation becomes real when the insights you've gained begin shaping your daily choices, your relationships, your self-talk, and your internal sense of stability. This is the chapter where healing stops being theoretical and becomes embodied.

Integration is the bridge between inner change and outward expression. It is the phase where awareness evolves into identity, and identity becomes action.

Many people reach a point in their healing where they understand their wounds, can name their patterns, and feel emotionally stronger, yet still struggle to live differently. This is not failure; it is simply the place where healing requires a deeper level of intentionality. Integration asks you to align your behaviors with your truth, your boundaries with your worth, and your decisions with your purpose.

Living from your healed self means allowing the work you've done to take root in the real world. It means practicing emotional regulation in moments that once overwhelmed you, choosing relationships that honor your growth, and making decisions that reflect your values rather than your fears. It means noticing old triggers but responding with new strength. It means holding yourself accountable without abandoning yourself emotionally. And it means embracing a life that feels aligned rather than familiar.

Integration also requires patience. You are learning to navigate life with a new internal compass, one built on truth, clarity, and self-respect instead of mere survival. Just as the body needs time to adjust after physical healing, the emotional self needs time to adjust to its new identity. Old patterns may resurface not because you are failing, but because the nervous system is learning that safety can exist without hypervigilance, chaos, or self-sacrifice.

This chapter is about learning how to stabilize your healing:

How to anchor your growth so deeply that it becomes part of your character, not just part of your story.

How to show up consistently as the version of yourself you have fought to remember.

How to build a life that can hold your new strength without collapsing into old wounds.

Here, you will explore:

- How to embody your healing in real-time decision-making
- How to replace emotional reflexes with intentional responses
- How to strengthen the habits that support growth
- How to create consistency between who you are privately and who you are publicly
- How to recognize when old patterns are resurfacing and gently redirect yourself
- How to cultivate internal balance as your identity evolves
- How to build a life that honors your purpose, peace, and emotional autonomy

Integration is where healing becomes a lifestyle.

Where strength becomes second nature.

Where peace shifts from being an aspiration to your default state.

Where you realize you are no longer living as the version of yourself who fought to survive, but as the version ready to thrive.

This chapter marks the moment you stop merely discovering who you are and start living it.

Embodying the Healed Self

Embodying the healed self is not about becoming someone different, it is about finally allowing yourself to live as the version of you that healing has been preparing all along. After years of survival-mode thinking, emotional restructuring, and intentional self-awareness, there comes a moment when something shifts. You begin not only to understand your healing, but to inhabit it. Healing moves from an internal concept to an outward expression. Your choices start reflecting your growth. Your responses begin to align with your wisdom. And your life begins to mirror the clarity you worked so hard to cultivate.

Embodying the healed self means moving through the world with authenticity instead of fear, intention instead of impulse, and inner steadiness instead of emotional chaos. It is the realization that healing is no longer just something you practice, it is something you are. You become more grounded, more aware, and more aligned. You trust your intuition, honor your limits, and no longer negotiate your worth for acceptance or approval.

But embodiment doesn't happen overnight. It unfolds gradually, in moments when you choose peace over panic, clarity over confusion, and truth over old narratives. It reveals itself in how gently you speak to yourself, how confidently you express your needs, and how firmly you stand in the direction your life is called to move. Embodiment is evident the first time you set a boundary without guilt, walk away from a familiar but unhealthy pattern, or choose silence over a reaction that once felt automatic.

This stage of your journey is about integration. It is where everything you've learned, released, and nurtured comes together to form a new way of being. You are no longer fragmented by your history. You are no longer defined by your wounds. Instead, you step into a fuller, more coherent version of yourself, one where your trauma story no longer leads the narrative. Embodiment requires courage, consistency, and compassion for the days when your old patterns call you back. But it also brings a profound sense of freedom: the freedom to move, speak, love, and show up from your healed center.

Most importantly, embodying the healed self means you stop waiting for permission. You stop shrinking. You stop apologizing for your existence, your voice, your power, or your evolution. You begin to show up as someone who knows they belong, not because the world told you so, but because healing taught you so. This is the chapter where your inner transformation becomes visible. This is where the healed self steps out of the shadows and into the fullness of who you were always meant to be.

Living From a Place of Inner Wholeness

Living from a place of inner wholeness means moving through the world anchored in who you truly are, rather than who you were taught to be. It is the shift from reacting to life to consciously engaging with it. When you embody your healed self, your decisions reflect your values rather than your wounds, your boundaries reflect your worth rather than your fear, and your relationships reflect your growth rather than your history.

Wholeness does not mean perfection. It does not mean that triggers disappear or that emotions become effortless. Instead, inner wholeness is a commitment to return to yourself, repeatedly, no matter what challenges arise. It is the understanding that you are defined not by fragmentation, but by integration. Every part of your story has a place, but no part of your story has permission to lead you away from your truth.

Living from wholeness means choosing alignment even when discomfort arises. You no longer shrink to fit outdated expectations or silence your voice to maintain connection. You stop negotiating your worth for temporary acceptance. Instead, you find stability in your authenticity, knowing that you no longer need to be chosen by others in order to choose yourself.

As inner wholeness strengthens, so does your emotional clarity. You recognize when an emotion is rooted in the present moment versus when it echoes from the past. You pause before reacting, listen inward before responding outward, and allow your intuition to guide you rather than fear, shame, or insecurity. This creates a life marked by intention and emotional sovereignty, a life where you lead from awareness rather than survival.

Wholeness also deepens your relationships. You begin to connect with others in ways that feel nourishing rather than draining. You choose people who honor your growth, support your boundaries, and celebrate your becoming. And when relationships shift or fall away, you navigate the transition without losing yourself. You learn that loss does not diminish your identity; it simply redirects your alignment.

Living from inner wholeness transforms the quality of your self-talk. Your inner dialogue becomes more compassionate, grounded, and reflective of the healing you've cultivated. You speak to yourself with honesty and kindness, replacing old narratives of inadequacy with ones rooted in empowerment and truth. You learn to affirm your progress, acknowledge your effort, and honor your journey not out of ego, but out of respect for the courageous work unfolding within you.

Most importantly, inner wholeness gives you the freedom to imagine and pursue a future that aligns with your highest self. You no longer make decisions solely to avoid pain or prevent rejection. Instead, you make choices that support your purpose, honor your growth, and reflect your deepest desires. You stop waiting to feel "ready" and begin trusting that your healing has prepared you for the life you are stepping into.

Wholeness is not a destination.

It is a way of being steady, intentional, rooted, and awake.

You become someone who no longer lives through the lens of "what happened to me," but through the clarity of "who I am now."

And that shift changes everything.

Integrating Wisdom into Daily Life

Healing becomes truly transformative when it moves beyond insight and becomes a lived experience. Knowledge without application remains dormant, but wisdom the kind gained through struggle, reflection, and emotional growth is meant to shape how you show up in the world each day. Integrating wisdom into daily life means allowing what you have learned about yourself to guide your choices, reactions, relationships, and the energy you allow into your life. It is the shift from understanding healing to embodying healing.

Wisdom integration begins with awareness. You start noticing the subtle moments when old patterns try to resurface, and instead of returning to familiar habits, you apply the truths you've worked hard to uncover. You pause before reacting. You choose honesty over avoidance. You respond with clarity rather than fear. You acknowledge your emotions without being ruled by them. This is how healing becomes practical, in the small decisions that shape the rhythm of your day.

At this stage, you begin to trust yourself more deeply. You no longer outsource your worth to other people's opinions or validation. Instead, you ground yourself in what you know to be true about who you are and the person you are becoming. Your self-awareness guides your boundaries. Your compassion guides your communication. Your values guide your direction. Wisdom becomes your internal compass, gently redirecting you toward alignment whenever life attempts to pull you off course.

Integrating wisdom also means living with intention. It is choosing relationships that nourish your spirit rather than drain it, environments that support your growth rather than stagnate it, and habits that reinforce your emotional and spiritual well-being. It is recognizing that every day offers an opportunity to practice what you have learned, to speak kindly to yourself, honor your needs, rest when you are tired, address discomfort rather than suppress it, and choose peace even when old chaos calls you back.

This integration extends to how you view challenges. Instead of seeing setbacks as proof of failure, you recognize them as invitations to deepen your awareness. Instead of collapsing under emotional triggers, you use them as signals guiding you toward unmet needs. Instead of fearing your past, you see how it has equipped you with resilience, empathy, and insight. Wisdom transforms obstacles into stepping-stones and pain into perspective.

As your wisdom integrates, life begins to feel different, not because it becomes easier, but because you navigate it with greater internal stability. You trust your intuition. You honor your truth. You move with purpose. You care for yourself with consistency. You allow relationships to evolve naturally and release what no longer aligns. The healed self does not require perfection; it requires presence. Wisdom keeps you present, rooted in truth, grounded in self-awareness, and connected to the journey you've worked so hard to walk.

Integrating wisdom into daily life is the final bridge between healing and wholeness. It is the moment your growth becomes visible not just in your thoughts, but in your choices. Not just in your insight, but in your embodiment. This is where transformation becomes lifestyle, where who you are becoming is reflected in how you live.

As you arrive at the end of this chapter, you stand in a place you once wondered if you would ever reach, the place where healing is no longer just something you pursue, but something you live. Embodying the healed self is not about becoming a perfect version of who you think you should be; it is about aligning with who you truly are. It is the quiet confidence that grows from every truth you've faced, every boundary you've honored, every layer of conditioning you've released, and every step you've taken toward emotional freedom. Integrating wisdom into daily life requires intention, patience, and presence. It is choosing alignment even on difficult days, choosing compassion when old triggers appear, choosing authenticity when the pull to perform resurfaces, and choosing growth when familiarity calls you back into who you used to be.

Healing has now woven itself into your choices, your values, your relationships, and your view of yourself. You are no longer defined by survival or limited by the voices of your past. You walk with an inner steadiness that cannot be shaken by old narratives or past wounds. You have reclaimed your identity, restored your sense of worth, and rewritten the story you once inherited. And while the journey of healing is ongoing, you now carry the tools, clarity, and emotional grounding to continue evolving with strength and grace.

Most importantly, you have become the safe place you always needed.

You have become the healed version of yourself that once felt out of reach.

You have become the author of your own becoming.

As you move forward, may you carry this truth with you:
Healing is not simply about what you leave behind, it is about who you rise into.

And you are rising beautifully.

CHAPTER 8
The Becoming: Stepping Into Your Future Self

Healing is not only about releasing what once hurt you, but also about redefining how you see yourself moving forward. By the time you reach this chapter, you have peeled back the layers of old narratives, confronted the voices of your past, nurtured your emotional world, and begun constructing a life rooted in intention rather than mere survival. Now comes one of the most powerful steps in your transformation: rewriting the internal vision of who you truly are.

From a young age, I learned a principle that would later shape my healing: to bring a vision full circle, you must first write it down, make it plain, and add faith until that faith becomes belief. This practice was not just about goals or dreams; it became a blueprint for identity. The same principle applies to how we view ourselves. To evolve, we must be willing to erase the distorted, disruptive images created by trauma, criticism, or emotional abandonment and replace them with the truest version of who we believe ourselves to be.

Self-vision is powerful. It directs your choices, influences your relationships, shapes your emotional patterns, and determines the limits you either honor or break. When trauma damages that vision, you begin seeing yourself through its residue, small, unworthy, incapable, or undeserving. But healing invites you to reclaim authorship. It asks you to rewrite your internal narrative with clarity, compassion, and truth.

This chapter is about consciously crafting the vision of your healed self, not the version shaped by fear, not the version shaped by judgment, not the version shaped by survival, but the version aligned with your purpose, your strength, and your rebirth. It is about seeing yourself through a lens of possibility rather than limitation.

Here, you begin the work of:

- Redefining your self-image based on truth rather than trauma
- Consciously choosing who you are becoming, rather than repeating who you were conditioned to be
- Identifying the beliefs that support your evolution and releasing the ones that restrict your growth

- Creating a future-oriented vision grounded in emotional freedom, spiritual alignment, and self-respect
- Understanding that transformation is sustained by intention, not by accident

Rewriting your self-vision is not wishful thinking. It is a disciplined act of emotional and spiritual alignment. It asks you to stand firmly in the truth: you are no longer defined by your past. The echoes of old voices and the residue of old wounds no longer bind you. You are now the creator of your identity, the narrator of your story, and the architect of your future.

In this chapter, consider a new question:

If you could see yourself clearly, free from the shadows of your past, who would you recognize?

The answer to that question is the starting point of your new vision. Write it, believe it, nurture it, and watch it begin shaping everything you are becoming.

Rewriting the Inner Narrative Through Self-Projection

One of the most overlooked truths in healing is this: the story you tell yourself about who you are becomes the blueprint for who you allow yourself to become. We often spend years absorbing others' opinions, judgments, and predictions about our lives, yet we rarely ask the most important question: What am I telling myself? The internal narrative you rehearse quietly wields more power than any words spoken over you.

We reflect on what others believe about our potential, yet we seldom examine the beliefs we project onto ourselves. If you want to be a doctor, are you creating an environment that nurtures that aspiration, or are you merely daydreaming from a distance? If you dream of becoming an astronaut, are you envisioning trips to NASA or the Space Center, or just watching videos about space while convincing yourself it's out of reach? What you expose yourself to shapes the inner message you repeat, and your actions reveal your beliefs long before your words do.

Self-projection is more than positive thinking it is the intentional act of aligning your internal narrative with the future you envision. It is choosing to tell a new story about who you are and who you are becoming. When your inner dialogue shifts, your behavior follows. When your behavior shifts, your life begins to reflect the identity you claim. This is the essence of rewriting your inner narrative: moving from passive wishing to active alignment.

Many of us internalized the predictions others made about us parents, teachers, peers. Their words became our script, replaying in moments of doubt or transition. But the healed self knows this vital truth: you are the author of your identity, not the echo of someone else's assumptions. Rewriting your inner narrative takes courage, honesty, and intention. It requires acknowledging your old story without letting it limit the new one.

Self-projection asks you to imagine yourself beyond the boundaries of your past and affirm that image until it becomes familiar. Project confidence before you fully feel it. Project capability before you have perfected it. Project worthiness even when traces of shame linger. Healing happens when your self-talk reflects potential, not pain.

The more you practice this, the more your actions will align with your aspirations. Dreams turn into plans. Possibility becomes direction. Identity expands. You stop living within inherited limitations and start living from intentional vision.

This is your invitation: examine the story you are projecting into your future.

Not the story others told you.

Not the one trauma tried to cement.

But the one you choose to write now,

with clarity, conviction, and belief.

Becoming the Version of Yourself You Believe In

Rewriting your inner narrative changes the way you think but embodying that narrative changes the way you live. Once you begin shifting what you believe about yourself, your actions will inevitably rise to meet that belief. Transformation cannot be sustained through thought alone, it requires aligned behavior, intentional choices, and the willingness to grow into the identity you are creating.

The version of yourself you are becoming is not shaped by chance; it is shaped by the daily decisions you make about who you are, what you deserve, and what you are willing to pursue. When your inner narrative evolves, your patterns must evolve with it. You cannot speak of empowerment while continuing to live in avoidance. You cannot declare confidence while shrinking in the presence of your calling. True change occurs when your actions reflect the truth you are claiming.

Becoming the version of yourself you believe in begins with clarity. You must know who you are becoming before you can live like that person. That clarity does not come from external approval; it comes from internal alignment. It is the moment you stop waiting for someone else to validate your potential and start validating it yourself. When you truly believe in who you are becoming, your behavior shifts from hesitation to intention, from doubt to preparation, from dreaming to building.

Every version of your future self requires action today:

If you want to be confident, practice speaking with conviction.

If you want to be disciplined, commit to consistency.

If you want to be emotionally grounded, practice emotional regulation.

If you want to be fulfilled, honor the desires that bring you alive.

Becoming is not instantaneous, it is incremental. It is the result of choosing, repeatedly, to align your thoughts, habits, environment, and energy with the identity you are embracing. Even small shifts create momentum. Every aligned choice tells your mind and spirit, "This is who I am now."

But becoming also requires honesty. You must be willing to release habits, relationships, and environments that contradict the future you are building. Growth cannot thrive where your old identity is reinforced. When you begin to believe in a higher version of yourself, it becomes impossible to remain committed to anything that diminishes your value or distracts you from purpose.

You become the version of yourself you believe in when you start showing up as that version, even before the external evidence appears.

Confidence comes before validation.

Action comes before opportunity.

Identity comes before manifestation.

This shift is powerful because it transforms your relationship with possibility. Instead of hoping for change, you begin preparing for it. Instead of waiting for doors to open, you start positioning yourself to walk through them. Instead of shrinking under old narratives, you expand into new ones.

Becoming is an act of faith, faith in your healing, in your growth, and in the self, you are choosing to become.

Visualizing Your Future Self

Visualization is one of the most transformative tools for emotional and personal growth. It allows you to see beyond your current limitations and into the version of yourself that is waiting to be embraced. When you intentionally envision the future you desire, you activate a powerful internal shift, one that moves you from uncertainty to alignment, from fear to possibility, and from doubt to purpose.

I mentioned earlier that I struggled with the idea of becoming a mental health professional because of my own emotional challenges. Even though I knew, from the time I was five, that this was my calling, the heaviness of my past and the voices of self-doubt made me question my worthiness. It wasn't until I realized that my struggles weren't disqualifications but qualifications that were the very experiences that equipped me to walk this path that everything changed. Once I embraced this truth, I began to see myself as the doctor I could become. I envisioned the degree, the work, the confidence, and the impact. Step by step, I walked toward the path that led me to success.

Visualization is not fantasy, it is preparation.

It is emotional rehearsal.

It is aligning your mind with the life you are building.

When you visualize your future self, you strengthen the neural pathways associated with success and confidence. You are no longer merely wishing for change; you are actively creating it from the inside out. Visualization becomes a source of encouragement, motivation, and empowerment, reminding you of what is possible when you dare to believe in your potential.

Seeing your future self clearly makes it easier to take aligned action. The more you envision the person you are becoming, how they think, how they carry themselves, how they love, how they lead, the more naturally you begin to embody those qualities in your daily life. Visualization becomes both a compass and a catalyst, guiding your choices and fueling your determination.

Your future self is not a distant dream.

They are a reflection of the truth within you, waiting for permission to emerge.

Becoming the Evidence of Your Future Self

There comes a moment in every healing and transformation journey when imagining your future self is no longer enough, you must begin becoming the evidence of that vision. Visualization plants the seed but aligned action nourishes it into reality. This is when belief shifts from an internal concept to outward expression, when who you are becoming begins to show up in how you live, speak, choose, and carry yourself.

The future you are envisioning is not created in a single grand moment; it is built quietly, through daily decisions that honor who you are growing into. Every choice becomes a vote for the person you wish to become. The more consistently you make choices aligned with your future self, the more natural that identity becomes. Transformation stops feeling like something you are striving for and begins to feel like something you are stepping into.

Becoming the evidence of your future self means asking, what would the healed, confident, empowered version of me do right now? It means aligning your habits with your intentions. It means speaking to yourself with the respect and compassion you want to embody. It means surrounding yourself with environments, people, and opportunities that reflect the direction your life is moving toward, not the direction you are leaving behind.

It also requires letting go of identities that no longer serve you. Sometimes the most challenging part of growth is releasing the familiar version of yourself you have outgrown. Even when that version was shaped by pain or misbelief, it can feel safer than stepping into the unknown. But becoming the evidence of your future self means trusting that the unknown is no longer a threat, it is an invitation.

This process is not about pretending to be someone you're not; it is about revealing the person you've always been beneath fear, doubt, and old narratives. Just as your past once shaped your self-perception, your intentional choices now shape your future identity. Every step you take in alignment with your vision strengthens your belief in what is possible.

The truth is your future self is not waiting for perfection; your future self is waiting for participation. Waiting on your willingness to shift. To choose differently. To rise above the old patterns that once held you in place. To show up as though the vision is already unfolding, because the moment you begin embodying it, it truly does.

Becoming the evidence of your future self is the bridge between who you were and who you are destined to be. It is where faith turns into movement, and movement into transformation. It is where alignment deepens into identity, and identity expands into purpose.

Your future self is not a fantasy.

It is a version of you that already exists waiting to be activated through your choices today.

Stepping Into the Future You Are Creating

As you arrive at the end of this chapter, you stand at the threshold of possibility a place where identity, intention, and imagination converge. By now, you have begun the courageous work of rewriting your inner narrative, challenging the perceptions that once confined you, and embracing the truth of who you are becoming. You have witnessed the power of seeing yourself beyond your past and projecting a version of yourself grounded in purpose, clarity, and faith.

Your future is not something that simply happens to you.

It is something you actively create.

Every vision you write down, every image you hold of yourself, every affirmation you repeat, and every step you take toward alignment shapes the life unfolding before you. You now understand that self-projection is not fantasy; it is a disciplined act of emotional, mental, and spiritual positioning. It is choosing to see beyond what is visible and believing in what is possible. It is erasing the distorted reflections produced by trauma and choosing to project the version of yourself that has always been there the resilient, capable, destined self-waiting to emerge.

You also recognize that your vision requires partnership with your faith, your discipline, your environment, and your willingness to grow. Your future self cannot be built on old narratives or limited by outdated beliefs. It requires intentionality, courage, and the willingness to step into unfamiliar territory with confidence.

As you continue on this journey, remember you are not simply rewriting your story, you are authoring new chapters through your choices, your thoughts, and your self-belief. Your vision is not fragile; it is powerful. It is the blueprint for who you are becoming and the compass that guides your steps.

Take a moment to honor the work you have done.

You have confronted your past, reimagined your present, and now you are beginning to design your future with purpose. This is not accidental growth; it is intentional transformation.

And as you step into the next chapter, hold onto this truth:

You are not defined by who you were.

You are defined by who you choose to become.

Your future is waiting not for perfection, but for presence.

Not for fear, but for faith.

Not for doubt, but for the unwavering belief that you are capable of rising into everything you have envisioned.

You have written the vision.

You have made it plain.

And now, you are becoming it.

CHAPTER 9
Walking In Your Becoming

There comes a moment in every healing journey when transformation shifts from something you think about to something you embody. Up to this point, you have examined your past, confronted internal narratives, nurtured your emotional world, rebuilt your identity, and learned to envision a future shaped by authenticity rather than survival. Now, in Chapter 9, you step into the lived expression of all that inner work, the phase where healing meets action.

Becoming is not a single moment of revelation; it is a continuous practice of choosing the version of yourself you have worked so hard to uncover. It means living in alignment with your truth even when old patterns try to pull you back. It means honoring your growth even when others still see a version of you that no longer exists. It means recognizing that your healing is not simply something you experienced, it is something you now carry into every interaction, decision, and direction of your life.

Walking in your becoming requires courage, consistency, and faith. It calls you to trust the path ahead even when it feels unfamiliar. It invites you to speak differently, think differently, respond differently, and choose differently, not because you are forcing change, but because you are finally aligned with who you were always meant to be.

This chapter is about living from your healed place, not your wounded one.

It is about stepping into opportunities you once doubted, embracing relationships you once feared, and showing up in spaces you once felt unworthy of entering.

It is about holding your head high, not because life has been easy, but because you survived what was meant to break you and rebuilt yourself from the inside out.

Chapter 9 teaches you how to:

- embody your healed identity in real time,
- practice resilience as a lifestyle rather than a reaction,
- make decisions rooted in clarity instead of fear,
- navigate life with confidence even when uncertainty arises,

- and walk boldly toward the future you once questioned.

This chapter marks a shift from internal work to external impact.

Your healing is no longer theoretical, it is visible.

It is lived.

It is active.

And most importantly, it is yours.

Up to this point, you have done the courageous work of returning to yourself: releasing the voices of your past, rewriting your inner narrative, practicing emotional nurturing, and choosing alignment over survival. Chapter 9 invites you into the next phase of healing, living intentionally in the life you are actively creating, not the one you inherited, endured, or settled for.

This chapter is about stepping forward with confidence, clarity, and emotional authority. It is about becoming an active participant in your future rather than a passive responder to your past.

Stepping Into the Life You Are Becoming

There comes a point in every healing journey when awareness turns into embodiment. You have examined your history, challenged your inner narratives, nurtured your emotional world, and begun rewriting the story you tell about yourself. Stepping into the life you are becoming marks an even deeper shift the moment you begin living as the person you have been healing to become.

This step forward is not a dramatic leap, but a series of intentional choices: quiet decisions and internal agreements that slowly shape your reality. It is choosing to show up differently, speak differently, think differently, and prioritize differently. It is allowing your healed identity to lead in moments where your wounded self once dictated your behavior.

This phase requires courage not loud, performative courage that seeks validation, but quiet courage rooted in daily choice. The courage to rise each morning and move with purpose. The courage to walk away from environments that no longer nourish you. The courage to embrace opportunities you once felt unworthy of. The courage to say yes to alignment and no to the patterns that once held you captive.

Stepping into your becoming also requires a shift in self-perception. Instead of viewing yourself through the lens of old wounds, you begin to see yourself through the lens of possibility. Instead of anticipating failure, you anticipate growth. Instead of questioning your worth, you act from a place of confidence and spiritual grounding. This shift does not happen overnight; it unfolds gently and consistently as you honor the version of yourself that is emerging.

At this stage, your internal dialogue becomes a powerful guide. You begin to speak to yourself as someone worthy of care, respect, and possibility. You stop minimizing your strengths and start acknowledging the gifts that have always been present. You recognize that healing has equipped you with resilience, clarity, and emotional intelligence, qualities that now shape the life you are building.

As you step more fully into your becoming, something remarkable happens: your external world begins to respond. The relationships you attract, the opportunities that arise, the boundaries you set, and the energy you carry all begin to realign with your healed identity. Life starts to reflect the work you have done within.

Stepping into the life you are becoming is not about perfection. It is about intention. It is about granting yourself permission to evolve, to expand, and to take up space in ways you once denied. It is a sacred transition, the bridge between who you have been and who you are meant to be.

This section invites you to move forward without apology, hesitation, or fear.

You are no longer defined by the wounds you carried.

You are defined by the strength and clarity that carried you through them.

Walking With Intention

Walking with intention means you are no longer drifting through life, waiting for clarity to arrive, you are choosing clarity through your actions, decisions, and mindset. Intention transforms healing from a private, internal evolution into a visible, external expression of who you are becoming.

When you walk with intention, your choices are no longer made from fear or habit; they are shaped by purpose. You begin making decisions that align with who you desire to be rather than who you used to be. You start choosing environments, relationships, habits, and opportunities that reflect your values and reinforce your growth. Intention becomes an internal compass, guiding you even when the path ahead is uncertain.

Healing is not proven by perfection it is proven by how intentionally you move through your life.

Intention is choosing peace over chaos.

Intention is choosing self-respect over self-sacrifice.

Intention is choosing long-term growth over temporary comfort.

Intention is choosing your future over your familiar past.

Every intentional step, no matter how small it may seem, becomes evidence that you are actively participating in your evolution. You are not waiting for change you are becoming the change.

Choosing Opportunities with Confidence: Opportunities That Reflect Your Healing

As you grow into the healed version of yourself, the opportunities you choose begin to shift. You no longer reach for what is merely familiar or convenient; instead, you choose what aligns with your worth, your growth, and your evolving identity. Choosing opportunities with confidence is not simply a matter of ambition, it is an act of self-recognition. It is the moment you acknowledge that you deserve the best options available to you, not just the ones you once believed were within reach.

Many of us grow up believing certain dreams are "too big," certain paths "not for people like us," or certain achievements reserved for others. These beliefs often stem from childhood messaging, limited environments, or experiences that taught us to shrink before we could imagine expanding. Healing challenges those narratives. It invites you to ask Why not me? instead of passively accepting Why me?

This shift from doubt to possibility lies at the heart of choosing opportunities that reflect your healing. When you begin to see yourself as capable, worthy, and equipped, the world opens in new ways. Doors you once overlooked become visible. Paths you once feared feel approachable. Possibilities you once dismissed become attainable.

Choosing opportunities with confidence also means understanding that what you desire is not accidental, it is a reflection of your purpose. If something has been placed on your heart, it is because you are meant to explore it. Your dreams are not fantasies; they are signals guiding you toward your potential. As you heal, you begin making decisions not from fear or scarcity, but from alignment and intention.

You start choosing roles, relationships, environments, and goals that mirror your growth rather than your wounds. You no longer settle for opportunities that require you to shrink, perform, or compromise your well-being. Instead, you gravitate toward what honors your value, challenges you to expand, and supports the person you are becoming.

Confidence, in this context, is not arrogance, it is clarity. It is the quiet assurance that you deserve to take up space, pursue purpose, and position yourself for success. It is the recognition that you are no longer bound by outdated limitations or old self-beliefs.

Choosing opportunities that reflect your healing means choosing abundance over fear, possibility over self-doubt, and self-worth over survival. It is a declaration that you are ready for more and that you finally believe you are worthy of it.

Walking Through the Doors You Once Believed Were Closed

Healing not only reshapes how you see yourself, but it also reshapes what you believe is possible for your life. Opportunities that once felt out of reach begin to feel attainable. Paths you once dismissed quietly reappear. Dreams you tucked away resurface with renewed meaning and strength. As your sense of self-worth deepens, so does your capacity to step into spaces you once believed you did not deserve.

Walking through new doors requires courage, awareness, and healed intention. This is not about forcing yourself into environments that do not align with your growth; it is about recognizing the doors that were always meant for you but were once obscured by self-doubt, fear, or unhealed narratives. Healing clears that lens. It teaches you to approach opportunities from a place of confidence and clarity rather than insecurity or scarcity.

One of the most profound realizations in this stage of healing is understanding that opportunities are not reserved for those who "have it all together." They are often claimed by those willing to grow into them. You do not need to be perfect to walk through a new door you only need to be willing.

This is where transformation becomes active. Instead of questioning your worthiness, you begin to question your hesitation. Instead of asking whether you belong, you ask how you can contribute. Instead of doubting your capability, you remind yourself of everything you have already survived. Healing teaches you that the same strength that carried you through pain can carry you into possibility.

Walking through new doors also requires discernment. Not every opportunity aligns with your healing, and not every invitation is meant to be accepted. But when a door reflects your growth, honors your identity, and draws you closer to your purpose, your responsibility is to step forward, even if your voice trembles.

This phase of growth is about becoming an active participant in your future. It is about trusting your readiness, honoring your preparation, and embracing your evolution. It is about refusing to retreat into old narratives and choosing instead to stand fully in the light of who you are now.

The doors you once believed were closed were never closed at all, you were simply becoming the version of yourself capable of walking through them.

Stepping Into Your Expansion

Healing is not only about reclaiming what was lost, but also about stepping boldly into what is now possible. By the time you reach this point in your journey, you have begun challenging internal limitations, expanding your sense of worthiness, and recognizing that opportunity is not reserved for a chosen few. It is available to anyone willing to see themselves as capable, deserving, and prepared.

This chapter invites you to view opportunity through a different lens, not as something distant or accidental, but as something you can intentionally choose. You learn that confidence is not arrogance; it is alignment. It is the quiet, steady belief that you are meant for more, that your presence matters, and that your story carries wisdom worth building upon. Each time you ask, "Why not me?" you dismantle the barriers that once kept you small.

As you integrate these truths, you begin to understand that choosing opportunity is choosing yourself. It is choosing a healed narrative over an old script, possibility over fear, and a life that reflects your internal transformation. You are no longer waiting for permission you are recognizing your readiness.

Opportunities that once felt out of reach now become invitations.

Dreams that once felt unrealistic now feel aligned.

Paths that once seemed impossible now appear designed for you.

This shift is not accidental. It is the result of your healing, the restructuring of your identity, beliefs, and emotional boundaries. As you heal, you no longer gravitate toward the familiar limitations of your past. Instead, you move toward environments, relationships, and futures that honor who you are becoming.

As you step forward, remember confidence is a practice, not a moment. Choosing opportunity is a muscle that strengthens with use. Believing in yourself is a commitment you renew each day. The more you trust your growth, the more your life expands to meet it.

Let this closing serve as a reminder:

You are no longer the person who questioned their value.

You are not bound by narratives that told you to stay small.

You are not limited by the fears that shaped your early story.

You are the architect of your future grounded, empowered, and capable of choosing opportunities that reflect your healing, your strength, and your unlimited potential.

Chapter 9 marks the beginning of a new way of living:

one where you walk with confidence, choose with intention, and step into expansion without apology.

You are ready for what comes next.

CHAPTER 10
Becoming The Author of Your New Story

There comes a point in healing when the past no longer feels like the defining force of your identity. You have examined your wounds, confronted inherited narratives, reclaimed your voice, nurtured your inner world, and stepped into alignment with the person you are becoming. By the time you reach this chapter, you are standing at the threshold of something profound, the realization that your story is no longer happening to you; it is unfolding through you.

Healing is not simply about recovery.

It is about authorship.

This chapter marks the transition from introspection to creation, from understanding your narrative to intentionally writing the next chapters of your life. Perhaps for the first time, you are no longer responding to the expectations of others, the echoes of your past, or the limitations of old beliefs. You are responding to yourself, to your purpose, your calling, and the unfolding truth of who you were always meant to be.

Becoming the author of your story means accepting that you have both the right and the responsibility to design a future that reflects your healing. It means recognizing that you are not bound to the character others cast you as. You are not confined to roles assigned during moments of pain. You are not obligated to continue narratives that were never yours to begin with.

Authorship is liberation.

It is permission.

It is reclaimed power.

And yet, it requires courage.

To author your life, you must be willing to release the old plot, the one shaped by survival, doubt, silence, and inherited pain. You must be willing to write with honesty, intention, and vision. You must dare to imagine a version of yourself no longer defined by wounds, but expanded by wisdom.

In this chapter, you will explore:

- How to release the remnants of outdated self-stories
- How to identify the themes, values, and truths that shape your new narrative
- How to consciously choose the direction of your emotional and spiritual evolution
- How to create a life that reflects not where you have been, but where you are going

This is the chapter where your healing becomes authorship where awareness becomes direction, and resilience becomes creation.

You have learned to see yourself.

You have learned to trust yourself.

Now you will learn to write yourself into the life you deserve.

Releasing the Old Narrative

Releasing the old narrative is one of the most essential steps in emotional and personal transformation. The stories we tell ourselves, often inherited from trauma, conditioned environments, or past failures, become invisible scripts that guide our behavior long after the moments that created them have passed. These narratives shape how we see ourselves, what we believe we deserve, and how we show up in the world. Healing, however, requires us to examine these internal scripts and decide which ones no longer belong in the life we are creating.

There is a commonly repeated saying that the definition of insanity is doing the same thing over and over while expecting a different result. Whether or not this was Einstein's original intent, the principle remains relevant: repetitive behaviors rooted in outdated beliefs cannot produce new outcomes. When we continue to live according to narratives shaped by pain, limitation, or former identities, we unconsciously recreate the very emotional experiences we are trying to escape. In this way, clinging to harmful narratives becomes a form of self-sabotage.

This reflection reveals a clear truth: releasing the old narrative is not optional, it is central to transformation. You cannot evolve while holding tightly to a version of yourself shaped by survival. You cannot expand while carrying stories that confine you. Letting go of old narratives means examining the roles you were assigned, the labels you accepted, and the beliefs that grew out of pain rather than truth. It requires questioning whether the identity you operate from today is genuinely yours or a reflection of what others projected onto you.

Releasing the old narrative does not erase your past; it liberates your future. It creates space for a new internal story, one grounded in self-awareness, compassion, and empowerment. When you release the narratives that kept you small, you reclaim the power to choose who you are becoming rather than remaining trapped in who you were told you were. This is the beginning of emotional freedom: the moment you decide that the story that once defined you no longer determines your destiny.

Reclaiming Your Truth and Writing a New Internal Story

Once you begin releasing the old narrative the beliefs, patterns, and emotional habits that no longer support your growth you create space for something profoundly transformative: the reclamation of your truth. Healing is not only about letting go; it is also about intentionally choosing what you allow to replace what has been released.

A new internal story does not write itself. It is shaped by your awareness, your courage, and your willingness to see yourself through a clearer, more compassionate lens. After years of surviving under narratives imposed by trauma, culture, family, or fear, reclaiming your truth becomes an act of liberation. For the first time, you decide the meaning of your experiences, the direction of your future, and the identity you will carry forward.

Reclaiming your truth requires honesty, the kind that asks you to see yourself without the distortion of shame or the weight of old wounds. It invites you to explore the strengths you once minimized, the potential you dismissed, and the purpose you were taught to doubt. In this stage, you allow yourself to recognize what has always been present but often overlooked: your resilience, your intelligence, your intuition, your compassion, and your capacity to evolve.

Writing a new internal story also demands intentionality. When you have spent years repeating unhelpful messages, I'm not enough. I always fail. I can't change. This is just who I am, those thoughts can feel automatic, familiar, and convincing. Changing them is not instantaneous; it is a practice. It requires choosing new messages, new interpretations, and new meaning again and again until they become the dominant narrative.

Your new story is not a fantasy or a denial of your past.

It is a declaration that your past no longer defines your identity.

You begin to replace limiting beliefs with narratives rooted in truth:

- Your worth is not determined by your wounds.
- Your potential is not limited by where you began.
- Your identity is not confined to who you were in your hardest seasons.
- Your future is not a repetition of your past unless you allow it to be.

Reclaiming your truth also means taking ownership of your voice. For many, trauma or emotional conditioning has silenced their sense of agency. They learned to defer, minimize, or filter themselves to maintain peace or avoid conflict. Writing a new narrative invites you to speak from a place of clarity and confidence rather than fear. You begin to trust your judgment, honor your emotions, and advocate for your needs without apology.

As you craft your new internal story, you will notice a shift. You no longer anchor your identity in pain. You no longer define yourself by the opinions of those who underestimated you. You begin to see yourself as capable of growth, worthy of respect, and deserving of opportunities that align with your healing.

This is the essence of Chapter 10:

You cannot create a new life while holding on to an old story.

Reclaiming your truth is the bridge between who you were and who you are becoming. It is the moment you stop living in reaction to your past and start living in alignment with your purpose. Your new narrative becomes the foundation upon which your future will stand strong, intentional, and authentically yours.

Reclaiming the Narrative Through Intentional Living

Once you begin releasing the old stories that shaped your identity, a new responsibility emerges, choosing how you will live moving forward. Healing is not simply the removal of what no longer serves you; it is the intentional adoption of patterns, beliefs, and behaviors that reflect the person you are becoming. This is where transformation shifts from internal awareness to outward expression.

Intentional living means that every choice emotional, spiritual, relational, or practical aligns with your truth rather than your trauma. It means you no longer move unconsciously through life, repeating outdated patterns or engaging in reflexive habits rooted in survival. Instead, you begin choosing what nurtures you, strengthens you, and supports your evolution.

Reclaiming your narrative through intentional living begins with recognizing that you now have agency. You are no longer governed by the automatic responses that once dictated your decisions. Your past may have influenced you, but it does not have the authority to script your future unless you give it permission.

Living intentionally calls for clarity:

What do you value?

What do you desire?

What do you want your emotional life to feel like?

What kind of relationships do you want to cultivate?

What environments help you thrive rather than shrink?

As you answer these questions, your daily decisions begin to shift accordingly. You start speaking with purpose instead of fear. You choose environments that honor your growth rather than recreate your wounds. You engage in relationships that support your healing and release connections that echo past dysfunction.

Intentional living also requires patience. Old patterns may resurface, not because you have failed, but because the mind gravitates toward what it knows. With each intentional choice, you retrain your emotional reflexes to follow your healed identity instead of your former narrative. You create new pathways, new responses, and new possibilities.

This process reinforces an essential truth:

Your life is no longer a reflection of what hurt you, it is an expression of who you are intentionally becoming.

As you reclaim your narrative through conscious living, you embody the freedom that comes from choosing yourself again. You step into a life that feels aligned, grounded, and authentic. Gradually, the remnants of your old narrative fade, replaced by a story you have crafted with resilience, clarity, and purpose.

Stepping Into Freedom Through Letting Go

Releasing old narratives is not merely an act of forgetting, it is an intentional choice to stop allowing outdated stories to dictate your present reality. Letting go requires courage because the narratives we cling to often feel familiar, even when they are painful. They offer predictability, a known script, and a well-worn emotional path. But healing asks you to choose freedom over familiarity.

Letting go means acknowledging that the version of yourself built for survival cannot lead you into the life you are creating now. It means no longer rehearsing the limitations others placed on you, no longer entertaining thoughts that diminish your worth, and no longer feeding beliefs born from trauma rather than truth.

This process is neither fast nor linear. Some days, letting go will feel empowering; other days, it may feel like loss. But with each release, each outdated belief, each internalized criticism, each fear that no longer aligns with your identity, you make space for clarity, abundance, and emotional expansion.

Letting go does not mean erasing the past. It means refusing to let the past dictate your future.

It means recognizing when a belief no longer reflects your growth.

It means choosing healing even when your history tries to pull you back.

It means embracing the discomfort of the unknown because you trust the person you are becoming.

Most importantly, letting go means giving yourself permission to evolve without guilt or apology. You are allowed to break patterns your family accepted. You are allowed to outgrow environments that once shaped you. You are allowed to choose peace over chaos, truth over fear, and purpose over pain.

Letting go is not a single moment. It is a spiritual, emotional, and mental practice that rebuilds your identity from the inside out.

With each release, you reclaim a piece of yourself that trauma once tried to take.

CHAPTER 11

Closing: Stepping Into the Freedom You Have Created

As this chapter closes, you stand in a powerful place, the space between who you were and who you are becoming. You have confronted old narratives, challenged generational beliefs, questioned emotional defaults, and learned the importance of releasing what no longer serves your highest good. You are beginning to understand that freedom is not found in rewriting your past, but in reinterpreting it with wisdom and compassion.

Releasing old narratives is not about erasing your story; it is about reclaiming authorship. The thoughts you repeat, the beliefs you carry, and the patterns you hold are not fixed. They are choices, choices you are now empowered to change. The moment you stop rehearsing the past is the moment you begin creating a new emotional language for your life.

Letting go is an act of self-respect. It is a declaration that you will no longer be defined by wounds you did not choose, circumstances you have outgrown, or expectations that never aligned with your truth. You are giving yourself permission to step into mental freedom, emotional authenticity, and spiritual alignment. This is the freedom that comes from awareness, the freedom that comes from choosing yourself.

As you move forward, remember this:

You are not breaking away from your past you are breaking open.

Breaking open to clarity.

Breaking open to purpose.

Breaking open to a life that reflects the healed version of you.

You have released what was.

Now, you are ready to embrace what can be.

EPILOGUE
The Becoming

Healing is never a straight line. It bends, circles, pauses, and accelerates in ways we don't always expect. But every step, every layer, every truth uncovered has brought you here, to the threshold of becoming. As you close this book, you are not ending your journey; you are stepping into a deeper awareness of who you are and who you are called to be.

You have walked through memory, reflection, truth, and transformation. You have faced the echoes of your past while reclaiming the power of your present. You have unlearned the narratives that wounded you and rebuilt those that strengthen you. And in doing so, you have proven one of the greatest truths about healing:

You were never broken, you were becoming.

The world may have taught you silence, but you found your voice.

Life may have offered limitations, but you discovered possibility.

Pain may have tried to define you, but you chose to define yourself.

This journey was not simply about overcoming trauma; it was about rediscovering wholeness. It was about meeting the parts of yourself hidden beneath fear, shame, and survival, and welcoming them back into the light with compassion.

You learned that resilience is not the absence of pain; it is the presence of persistence.

You learned that healing is not about erasing your past; it is about transforming your relationship to it.

You learned that the power to rebuild, redefine, and rise has always lived within you.

Spiritually, emotionally, and psychologically, you now stand in a place of alignment, where faith meets action, insight meets intention, and your inner truth finally has room to breathe.

As you move forward, remember:

You are allowed to evolve beyond the person your trauma created.

You are allowed to rewrite the narrative you once believed.

You are allowed to be both a masterpiece and a work in progress.

Your journey does not end here. This is only a beginning, a new chapter shaped not by fear, but by clarity; not by woundedness, but by wisdom; not by survival, but by purpose.

Hold onto the tools you've gained.

Return to the reflections that grounded you.

Nurture the voice you worked so hard to find.

Trust that every step ahead is guided by the healed and healing version of you.

You have become the author of your story not merely the survivor of it.

And as you continue writing the next chapters of your life, may each page remind you of the truths you uncovered here:

You are worthy.

You are capable.

You are becoming.

Your journey, your unique journey is far from over.

ACKNOWLEDGMENTS

This book is a testament to the power of reflection, resilience, and the quiet strength that grows in the spaces where healing takes root. Although the journey toward self-awareness is deeply personal, I did not walk it alone. It was shaped, nurtured, and supported by the people whose presence, love, and influence formed the foundation from which I could rise.

To my family, thank you for being the first architects of my story. To my grandmother, whose gentle reminders of my worth carried me through seasons when I struggled to believe in myself, your voice became the anchor that grounded me. You taught me the importance of legacy, of knowing where I come from, and of standing firmly in who I am becoming. Your belief in my potential gave me courage long before I had the words to name it.

To my children and loved ones who witnessed my evolution, thank you for your patience, your love, and the quiet ways you motivated me to keep going. You are each a reminder that healing is not only for ourselves but for the generations that follow.

To the mentors, teachers, and therapists who poured into my growth, your wisdom helped me understand the value of emotional truth, the necessity of reflection, and the beauty of choosing authenticity over performance. You offered guidance during moments when the path felt uncertain, and your encouragement shaped the personal and professional growth reflected throughout these pages.

To the readers who find pieces of themselves within this book, thank you. Thank you for being brave enough to sit with your truth, open enough to explore your inner world, and committed enough to walk toward healing with intention. Whether your journey mirrors mine or unfolds in entirely different ways, your willingness to grow is sacred. May these words meet you exactly where you are and accompany you as you move toward where you are destined to be.

To every version of myself that survived so I could write these words, I honor you. You endured what you were never meant to carry, yet you continued to rise. You learned, you questioned, you broke, and you rebuilt. This book is as much your testimony as it is your triumph.

And finally, to God thank You for the grace that carried me, the strength that sustained me, and the clarity that guided me. Every chapter of my life has been touched by Your hand, and this work would not exist without Your presence illuminating my steps.

With gratitude, humility, and a heart transformed,

Thank you.

ABOUT THE AUTHOR

Chanter Simmons is a dedicated mental health professional, entrepreneur, educator, and advocate for emotional wellness and personal transformation. Guided by her own lived experiences, she has devoted her career to helping individuals heal the unseen wounds that shape identity, relationships, and the journey toward self-awareness.

From an early age, Chanter felt called to the world of counseling and emotional support, even before fully understanding the challenges she would face. Growing up in a large, blended family, she experienced firsthand how trauma, silence, and internalized narratives can shape a person's sense of self. Rather than allowing these experiences to define her limitations, she transformed them into her greatest qualifications, the foundation of her empathy, insight, and therapeutic wisdom.

Chanter is the founder of Grace & Mercy Therapeutic Resolutions, a brand committed to mental health empowerment, emotional resilience, and healing through truth-telling and self-recognition. Through her work, she blends clinical expertise with a profound understanding of human vulnerability, offering a compassionate pathway toward emotional restoration and wholeness.

In addition to her clinical and educational contributions, Chanter is a successful multi-business entrepreneur, with ventures spanning mental health, tax solutions, business development, and community-centered leadership. Her diverse professional footprint reflects her belief that healing and empowerment should extend beyond the therapy room and into every area of life.

Imprints of the Past: The Journey to Self-Awareness and Resilience is a deeply personal extension of her mission, helping individuals rewrite narratives that once restricted them and embrace the identities they were always meant to embody. Drawing from her own breakthroughs and the countless stories of those she has supported, Chanter writes with honesty, clarity, and compassion, offering readers not just guidance but genuine companionship on their healing journey.

Chanter continues her doctoral work in psychology, expanding her research on emotional development, trauma-informed care, and the integration of mental health practices in modern therapeutic settings. Her commitment to service, healing, and faith-driven purpose remains at the heart of everything she creates.

She resides in Georgia and is a proud mother, leader, and visionary, with a life's work rooted in empowering others to rise above their past and walk boldly into their purpose.

www.ingramcontent.com/pod-product-compliance
Lightning Source LLC
Chambersburg PA
CBHW031124160426
43192CB00008B/1105